THE CHILD AND THE OUTSIDE WORLD

STUDIES IN DEVELOPING RELATIONSHIPS

by D. W. Winnicott

THE CHILD AND THE FAMILY

D. W. WINNICOTT

The Child
and the
Outside World

Studies in Developing
Relationships

EDITED BY

JANET HARDENBERG
M.B.

TAVISTOCK PUBLICATIONS LTD

First published in 1957
by Tavistock Publications Limited
2 Beaumont Street, London, W. 1

Printed in Great Britain
in 11-point Baskerville by
Bradford & Dickens, London

EDITOR'S NOTE

THIS book is a companion volume to *The Child and the Family*, by the same author, which consists mainly of talks to parents about their young children in the setting of the normal home. Here are collected together writings concerned chiefly with the older child addressed to teachers and case workers. Over a period of years, some of these have been broadcast, others have appeared in various periodicals ; some have not previously been published. The date and the source of first publication or broadcast have wherever possible been given.

One might ask the reason for republishing wartime broadcasts on problems connected with the mass evacuation of children from the danger areas. Though these conditions have passed, the problems of separation remain ; and these talks make a valuable contribution to their study. They also constitute, in a sense, a tribute—a 'lest we forget' —to those parents, foster-parents, and children who did manage to make a success of a very difficult task. Some of those who will read this book were themselves children during the last war and may have had their own experience, good or bad, of evacuation. The chapter on residential management as treatment for difficult children (written with Miss Clare Britton) is still relevant today and has historical as well as practical interest ; indeed it was on such reports that the findings of the Curtis Committee on the Care of Children, 1945–6, were based. Miss Britton and Dr. Winnicott were both witnesses before this Committee.

While this book is primarily addressed to those who are professionally concerned with the care of children, it will also be read by interested parents who have found stimulation and guidance in Dr. Winnicott's first book, to which this volume, although complete in itself, is a sequel.

JANET HARDENBERG, M.B.

ACKNOWLEDGMENTS

Thanks are recorded to the following individuals and organisations for permission to publish material that has already appeared in print: the British Broadcasting Corporation; the Editor of the *British Journal of Medical Psychology*; the Editor of *Case Conference*; the Editor of *Delinquency Research*; the Editor of *Human Relations*; the Editor of the *Medical Press*; the Editor of the *National Froebel Foundation Bulletin*; the Editor of the *New Era in Home and School*; the Editor of the *Nursery Journal*; the Editor of the *Practitioner*; and the United Nations Educational, Scientific, and Cultural Organisation.

CONTENTS

EDITOR'S NOTE   *page* vii

ACKNOWLEDGMENTS   viii

PART I. THE CARE OF GROWING CHILDREN

1. *Needs of the Under-Fives in a Changing Society*   3
   Published in the *Nursery Journal*, vol. XLIV, no. 396,
   p. 15, June 1954

2. *The Child's Needs and the Role of the Mother
   in the Early Stages*   14
   An excerpt from *Mental Hygiene in the Nursery
   School:* Report of a joint W.H.O.-U.N.E.S.C.O. Expert
   Meeting held in Paris, September 1951; published by
   U.N.E.S.C.O. as no. IX in the series *Problems in
   Education,* 1953. Written in conjunction with other
   members of the group

3. *On Influencing and Being Influenced*   24
   Published in the *New Era in Home and School*, vol.
   22, no. 6, p. 118, 1941

4. *Educational Diagnosis*   29
   Published in the *National Froebel Foundation Bulletin*,
   no. 41, p. 3, September 1946

5. *Shyness and Nervous Disorders in Children*   35
   Published in the *New Era in Home and School*, vol.
   19, no. 7, p. 189, 1938

6. *Sex Education in Schools*   40
   Published in the *Medical Press*, vol. CCXXII, no.
   5761, October 1949

7. *Pitfalls in Adoption*   45
   Published in the *Medical Press*, vol. CCXXXII, no.
   6031, December 1954

8. *Two Adopted Children*   52
   Published in *Case Conference*, December 1953

PART II. CHILDREN UNDER STRESS
(Including Wartime broadcasts)

1. *Children in the War*   69
   Published in the *New Era in Home and School*, vol.
   21, no. 9, p. 229, 1940

Contents

2. *The Deprived Mother*   75
   B.B.C. broadcast, 1939; published in the *New Era in
   Home and School,* vol. 21, no. 3, p. 64, 1940

3. *The Evacuated Child*   83
   B.B.C. broadcast, 1945

4. *The Return of the Evacuated Child*   88
   B.B.C. broadcast, 1945

5. *Home Again*   93
   B.B.C. broadcast, 1945

6. *Residential Management as Treatment for
   Difficult Children*   98
   Published in *Human Relations,* vol. 1, no. 1, p. 87,
   1947

7. *Children's Hostels in War and Peace*   117
   Published in the *British Journal of Medical Psychology,*
   vol. XXI, part 3, p. 175, 1948

PART III. REFLECTIONS ON IMPULSE
           IN CHILDREN

1. *Towards an Objective Study of Human Nature*   125
   Published in the *New Era in Home and School,* vol.
   26, no. 8, p. 179, 1945, under the title 'Talking about
   Psychology'; reissued in vol. 33, no. 3, p. 55, 1952,
   under the title 'What is Psycho-Analysis?'

2. *Further Thoughts on Babies as Persons*   134
   Published in the *New Era in Home and School,* vol.
   28, no. 10, p. 199, 1947, under the title 'Babies Are
   Persons'

3. *Breast Feeding*   141
   1945, revised in 1954

4. *Why Children Play*   149
   Published in the *New Era in Home and School,* vol.
   23, no. 1, p. 12, 1942

5. *The Child and Sex*   153
   Published in the *Practitioner,* vol. 158, p. 324, April
   1947

6. *Aggression*   167
   c. 1939

7. *The Impulse to Steal*   176
   1949

8. *Some Psychological Aspects of Juvenile
   Delinquency*   181
   Published in the *New Era in Home and School,* vol.
   27, no. 10, p. 295, 1946, and in *Delinquency Research,*
   vol. 24, no. 5

INDEX   188

PART I

The Care of
Growing Children

Needs of the Under-Fives in a Changing Society

W E all know that families are generally smaller than formerly, and that mothers of two or so children arrive at
the age of 40 with a thirty-five-year expectation of life,
and with plenty of energy and some experience. My particular job
is to study the needs of the under-fives in relation to this and other
changes. First I must ask the question: do these changes in the
society pattern affect the under-fives in any significant way? My
emphasis must be on the fact that the needs of infants and small
children are not variable, they are inherent and unalterable.

What are the needs of normal or healthy under-fives?

It is necessary to think all the time of the *developing* child. This
is always a helpful approach, but it is especially important in the
case of the under-fives since each child of 4 is also 3 and also 2
and also 1, and is also an infant being weaned or an infant just
born, or even an infant in the womb.

It is a long distance from the new-born babe to the five-year-old
child in terms of personality and emotional growth. This distance
cannot be covered except by the provision of certain conditions.
These conditions need only be good enough, since a child's intelligence becomes increasingly able to allow for failures and to deal
with frustrations by advance preparation. As is well known, the
conditions that are necessary for the child's individual growth are
themselves not static, set, and fixed, but are in a state of qualitative
and quantitative change relative to the infant's or the child's age
and changing needs.

Consider closely the healthy boy or girl of $4\frac{1}{2}$. In the course
of the day there can appear a degree of worldliness like that of
an adult. The boy has become able to identify with father and

3

the girl with mother, and there are also the cross-identifications. This capacity for identification shows in actual behaviour, and in the taking of responsibility for a limited time over a limited area; it shows in play in which the tasks and joys of married life, of parenthood and of pedagogy are plainly displayed; it shows in the violent loves and jealousies which are characteristic of the age; and it exists in the day fantasies and especially and fundamentally in the dreams of the child asleep.

These are some of the mature elements in the healthy four-year-old, especially taking into consideration the intensity of living that derives from the child's *instinct*, the biological basis for excitements that show the sequence : preparation with increasing tension, climax, and then a measure of relaxation following some form of gratification.

In the full-blooded dream that marks the maturity that belongs to the period just before 5 or so, the child is at one apex of a triangle in human relationships. In this full-blooded dream the biological drive which we call instinct is accepted, and it is no mean feat for an individual child to keep up with biological growth, so that in the dream, and in the potential fantasy behind waking life, the child's bodily functions are involved in relationships of intense kind, with love felt as such, and also hate, and also the conflicts which are inherent in human experience.

A need of the well developed four-year-old is to have parents with whom to identify. At this important age it is no good implanting morals and inculcating cultural patterns. The operative factor is the parent, and the parent's behaviour, and the two parents' inter-relationship as perceived by the child. / It is this that the child takes in, and imitates or reacts against, and it is this also that the child uses in a hundred ways in the personal process of self-development. /

Moreover, the home, which has as its basis the relationship between the parents, has a function to perform by existing and by surviving; the child's expressed hate, and the hate that appears in the disasters of dreams, can be tolerated by the child because of the fact that the home continues to function in spite of the worst and because of the best.

But a child who is at times amazingly mature at $4\frac{1}{2}$ suddenly becomes a two-year-old when in need of reassurance because of a

4

cut finger or a chance fall, and is liable to become quite infantile at the time of going off to sleep. A child of any age who needs to be held affectionately needs a physical form of loving which was naturally given by the mother when she carried her infant in her womb.

Indeed, the infant does not start off as a person able to identify with other people. There has had to be a gradual building up of the self as a whole or a unit, and there has to be a gradual development of the capacity to feel that the world outside and also the world within are related things, but not the same as the self, the self that is individual and peculiar and never the same in two children.

The attainment of a maturity appropriate to the age between 3 and 5 is emphasised first, because healthy infants and children are all the time building up for this maturity that is so vital to the whole future development of the individual. At the same time the maturity of the under-five child is normally compatible with every kind and degree of immaturity. The immaturities are the residues of the earlier maturities—of the healthy states of dependence that are characteristic of all the earlier phases of growth. It is simpler to give soundings taken at the various phases of development than to attempt to paint the composite picture of the child of 4.

Even in a condensed statement one must separate out the following elements :

(1) Triangular relationship (held by the family).
(2) Two-person relationship (mother introducing the world to the baby).
(3) Mother holding infant in unintegrated state (seeing the whole person before the infant feels whole).
(4) Mother's love expressed in terms of physical management (maternal techniques).

(1) Triangular Relationship

The child has become a whole human being among whole human beings, caught up in triangular relationships. In the underlying or unconscious dream the child is in love with one parent and in consequence hates the other. To some extent the hate is expressed in direct form, and that child is lucky who can gather together all the latent aggressive residue from the earlier phases to use in this hating, which is acceptable because its basis is primitive love. To some extent, however, this hate is absorbed in the child's ability to identify with the rival in the dream. Here the family situation carries the child and the child's dream. The triangle has a reality form and this remains intact. The triangle is found also in all kinds of near relationships which allow a spreading out from the central theme and a gradual lessening of the tensions till they become just manageable in some real situation. Play is especially important here, since it is both real and also a dream, and although play experiences allow tremendous feelings of all kinds which otherwise stay locked up in the unremembered dream, the game eventually ceases, and those who are playing pack up and eat tea together, or prepare for bath and the bed-time story. Moreover, in play (at the period we are considering) there is always a grown-up person nearby who is indirectly involved, and who is ready to assume control.

A study of the two childhood games, fathers and mothers, and doctors and nurses, could easily be instructive to the newcomer to this subject, as well as the specific games based on the imitation of mother's work in the home and father's special job. Study of children's dreams demands special skill, but naturally takes the student farther into the unconscious than the simple observation of children's play.

(2) *Two-Person Relationship*

At an earlier stage, instead of the triangular relationship we get the more direct relationship between infant or small child and mother. In extremely subtle ways the mother is introducing the world to the baby, in limited ways, by warding off chance impingements, and by supplying what is needed more or less in the right way and at the right time. It can easily be seen that in this two-body relationship there is much less room (than in the triangular pattern) for the individual child's personal management of awkward moments; in other words there is greater dependence. Nevertheless there are two whole human beings, intimately interrelated, and interdependent. If the mother is herself healthy, not anxious, depressive, muddled, or withdrawn, then there is a wide scope for the growth of the small child's personality in the day-to-day enrichment of the infant-mother relationship.

(3) *Mother Holding Infant in Unintegrated State*

Earlier than this there is, of course, an even greater degree of dependence. The mother is needed as someone who survives each day, and who can integrate the various feelings, sensations, excitements, angers, griefs, etc. that go to make up an infant's life but which the infant cannot hold. The infant is not yet a unit. The mother is holding the infant, the human being in the making. The mother can, if necessary, go over in her mind all that the day has meant to the infant. She understands. She sees her infant as human at a time when the infant is incapable of feeling integrated.

(4) *Mother's Love Expressed in Terms of Physical Management*

Still earlier the mother is holding her infant, and this time I mean it physically. All the very early details of *physical* care are *psychological* matters for the infant. The mother makes an active adaptation to the infant's needs, and at the start this adaptation can be remarkably complete. The mother knows, instinctively as people say, what need is just about to become pressing. She presents the world to the infant in the only way that does not spell chaos, by the meeting of needs as they arise. Also by expressing love in terms of physical management and in the giving of physical satisfactions she enables the infant psyche to begin to live in the infant body. By her technique of infant care she expresses her feeling towards her infant, and builds herself up as a person who can be recognised by the developing individual.

This statement of needs is given as a basis for a discussion of the impact on the child of the various changes which have been observed in the family pattern. The needs each in their own way are absolute, taking into account their changing quality. Failure to meet such needs results in a distortion of the individual child's development, and it can be taken as an axiom that the more primitive the type of need the greater is the dependence of the individual on the environment, and the more disastrous the failure to meet such needs. The early management of an infant is a matter beyond conscious thought and deliberate intention. It is something that becomes possible only through *love*. We sometimes say the infant needs love, but we mean that only someone who loves the infant can make the necessary adaptation to need, and only someone who loves the infant can graduate a failure of adaptation to

7

follow the growth of the individual child's capacity to make positive use of adaptive failure.

The essential needs of the under-fives belong to the individuals concerned, and the basic principles do not change. This truth is applicable to human beings of the past, present, and future, anywhere in the world, and in any culture.

APPLICATIONS

In order to bring about a relationship between the idea of a changing family pattern and that of the needs of the under-fives it will be necessary to choose a few examples of change—for instance :

(1) Parents and their sense of job.
(2) Society and its sense of responsibility.
(3) Relative lack of siblings.

(1) *Parents and their Sense of Job*

There seems to be in young parents a new sense of doing a job to-day, and I start with this because it is one of those many important things that do not appear in statistical enquiry. Modern parents wait; they plan, and they read. They know they will be able to give proper attention only to two or three children, and so they set out to do their limited parental job in the best possible way. They do it themselves. The result, when all goes well, is a richness and a directness of relationship which is alarming in its intensity and richness. We expect, and find, special difficulties arising out of the lack of displacements. The triangle of parents and child becomes a reality indeed, and outside help is often required and can be usefully given.

It can be seen that parents who are so deliberately set on a job, that of starting their children off well on the road to mental health, are themselves individualists. It is part and parcel of this individualism that the parents themselves may later need to make further personal growth. In modern society there is a lessening of sham, and of the dress happiness, under the cloak of respectability.

These parents who feel they are on a job provide a rich setting for the infant and small child. Moreover, if real help is available such parents make use of it. But this help must not be of such a kind that it undermines the parents' sense of responsibility.

8

The birth of a new baby can be a valuable experience for the older child, or can be a great trouble, and parents who are willing to give time for consideration are able to avoid avoidable errors. However, it must not be expected that by taking thought we can prevent love, hate, and conflict of loyalties. Life is difficult and for no one more difficult than for the normal healthy child of 3 to 5. Fortunately life is rewarding also, and at this early age it holds out promise, provided the home feels stable, and the child gets the sensation of happiness and contentment in the parents' inter-relationship.

Parents who set out to be adequate parents certainly give themselves a big task, and there is always the risk that there will be no reward. Many chance circumstances may rob the parents of success (but fortunately there is much less risk from physical illness than there was twenty years ago). Parents are willing to study the needs of their children, and this helps; it must be remembered, however, that parents cannot love each other if things go wrong between them just because the children need them to be in stable relationship.

(2) *Society and its Sense of Responsibility*

There has been a vast change in society's attitude towards infant and child care. This came (naturally it had to) through the relatively false channels of rescue from physical sickness and from emotional deprivation, but now it begins to be found through a better motive, the understanding that in infancy and childhood is laid the basis for mental health and eventually for maturity in terms of the adult who can identify with society without loss of sense of self-importance.

Everywhere we find frantic attempts to switch workers over from treatment to prevention. There is a great danger here. Prevention of psychological troubles is not at all the same thing as the promotion of health. If we wish to promote health we must really know about the emotional development of the infant and child, and we must study psychological theory.

Examples might help to clarify the issue here. The great advances of paediatrics in the first half of this century have been mainly on the physical side. A well-known paediatrician said to me that he works on the principle 'better a live donkey than a dead horse'.

This means that if physical disease in a child can be prevented or cured the psychology of the child can be left to take care of itself. Paediatrics still needs to rise above this basic principle, and will have to find a way of doing so without losing grip on the care of physical health. The work of Dr. John Bowlby, who has concentrated on one thing, the ill effect on a small child of separation from the mother, has produced a very big change in procedure in the last few years, so that. mothers now visit their children in hospital, and wherever possible a separation is avoided. Moreover, there has been a change of policy in the management of deprived children, with a virtual abolition of the residential nursery and an increasing development of the use of the foster-home. But the paediatricians and nurses who co-operate in these matters are still lacking in true understanding of the reasons behind the small child's need for continuity of relationship with the mother and father. It is an important step forward, however, if it is recognised that much mental ill-health can be prevented by the avoidance of unnecessary separations. What is still needed is a better understanding of the building up of the child's mental health in the normal family setting.

Again, doctors and nurses know a great deal about the physical side of pregnancy and child-birth and about the infant's bodily health in the first months of life. They do not know about the bringing together of a mother and baby in the first feeds, however, because this is a delicate matter which is beyond rules and regulations, and only the mother herself can know how to do this. Very great distress is caused universally by interference by experts in other skills, just when the mother is finding her way with her baby at the start.

We need to see that the trained worker in the field (maternity nurse, health visitor, nursery school teacher, etc., each a specialist in a job) may be immature as compared with a father or mother, and the parents' *judgment* over a specific matter may be more sound than that of the worker. This need cause no difficulty if the point is understood. The trained worker is necessary because of his or her special knowledge and skill.

What parents need all along is enlightenment about underlying causes, not advice and not instruction as to procedure. Parents must also be given room for experiment and for making mistakes, so that they can learn.

The spread of social case work into the psychological field, which can immediately prove its value on the preventive side through the acceptance of broad principles of management, nevertheless provides a great threat to the normal or healthy family life. It is wise to remember that the health of the country depends on the healthy family units with parents who are emotionally mature individuals. These healthy families are therefore sacred territory, not to be entered except with real understanding of positive values. Nevertheless, the healthy family unit needs help from wider units. The parents are all the time engaged in their own personal interrelationship, and they are dependent on society for their own happiness and social integration.

(3) *Relative Lack of Siblings*

A significant change in the family pattern is the relative lack not only of brothers and sisters but also of cousins. Do not let us imagine that we can supply cousins by supplying playmates. Blood relationship is of extreme importance in the gradual displacement of the child's two-body and three-body relationships outwards from the mother, and the father and mother, to society in its wider aspect. It is to be expected that the modern child often has no help of the kind which was provided in the days of the large families. It must be common for a child to have no accessible cousin, and in the case of an only child this is a serious matter. Nevertheless, if this principle is accepted, we may say that the main help that can be given to the modern small family is in the extension of the range of relationship and opportunity. The nursery school, the nursery class, and the day nursery can do much, if not too big and if properly staffed. I refer not only to adequate staffing, but also to the education of staff in matters of infant and child psychology. Parents can use the nursery to give themselves a break; to enlarge the range of the infant's relationships both with adults and with other small children, and to enlarge the scope of playing.

Many normal or near-normal parents are irritable with their children if they have them all day and night, but if they have some hours to themselves they can be good with their child the rest of the time. I draw especial attention to this point, because in my practice I am always being confronted with the need for mothers to be helped when they seek part-time employment for the sake of their own health and equanimity. There is much room for argument here, but with regard to the healthy family (and I hope it will be accepted that this is not a rare phenomenon) the parents can take part in making variable decisions about nursery-school or day-nursery attendance. I would draw especial attention to this point of the parents' need for a break, and to plead for opportunity for use of day nurseries by mothers who are working only part-time. It has been pointed out to me that if there is a shortage of day nurseries, the alternative is not that the children stay with their mothers. Only this week I have seen a woman who was unable to make suitable contact with her own child and who has had fifty-two foster-children. She is unregistered and tells me that she dislikes interference. She has probably done a fairly good job in her own way, but it is impossible to assume that such foster-parents, self-styled, are as suitable as well organised and well staffed day nurseries.

It should be remembered that in this country education adapted to the nursery school has reached a very high standard. Our nursery schools have led the way in the world, partly through the influence of Margaret McMillan and my late friend Susan Isaacs. Moreover, the education of teachers for nursery-school work has affected the whole attitude towards teaching at later age groupings. It would be tragic indeed to see anything but further development of the sort of nursery school that is really suitable for giving help to the healthy family. The day nursery is of course at a disadvantage because, just as it existed during the war because of its value in the industrial world, when it was important to induce mothers to work in factories, so to-day the day nursery exists to cater for priorities, namely children with one parent only, unmarried mothers, deserted wives, deserted husbands, widows, widowers, also children of parents of whom one is ill (usually chronically) or disabled with a small pension. Investigation has shown that there is not enough room to accommodate the priorities, and there is no room at all left over for giving help to the healthy family. The day nursery is therefore not *primarily* designed for the infant, and the authorities that support it are not certain to be properly interested in staffing or equipment. The day nursery is more likely than the nursery school to be under the dominance of the medical authorities who, I am sorry to say, since I am a doctor, sometimes seem to think that the health of an individual is a matter of bodily growth and freedom from physical disease. Nevertheless the day nursery can do some of the work which a really good nursery school, properly staffed and equipped, is designed to do and, above all, can enable tired and worried mothers to be good enough mothers because they have had a change of occupation.

Day nurseries will continue to find official support because of their more obvious value to society in distress; let them be well equipped and staffed else they must do harm to the normal children of healthy families. The nursery school at its best is so good that the good family in modern times can use it for sensible extensions of the scope of otherwise lonely small children; and because the good nursery school caters for the healthy family it has a very special, though intangible, non-statistical value to the community. Society must have a future if the present is to be taken seriously, and out of the healthy family comes the future.

GENERAL SUMMARY

The needs of infants and small children are of such a nature that deliberate effort cannot meet them. It is better to start with the idea of the normal or healthy home in which the needs of each child are met by an environment that in itself develops with the child. Society must first of all recognise that the work of infant care and of the care of small children comes from love, so that the parents' job is recognised as one that is spoilt by interference. On this basis help can be given by the protection of the family from interference by provision of preventive and curative facilities on the physical side, by the provision of facilities for help and advice in the case of difficulty on the psychological side, and by the provision of something equivalent to the nursemaid and the nursery of the Victorian era. Along with all this goes a great need for a better understanding of the psychology of the child developing in the normal or healthy family, and of the earlier stages of infant development at the time of the infant's greatest dependence on the mother. The prophylaxis of mental and psycho-somatic disorders lies in the better understanding of the work of the healthy family, and of the healthily dependent infant, with the mother able and willing to play her part, not because she is clever or good but because the infant is hers.

2

The Child's Needs and the Role of the Mother in the Early Stages
[1951]

I N previous sections [of this report] it has been several times emphasised that the function of the nursery school is not to be a substitute for an absent mother, but to supplement and extend the role which in the child's earliest years the mother alone plays. In other words, the nursery school is probably most correctly considered as an extension 'upward' of the family, rather than an extension 'downward' of the primary school. It seems desirable, therefore, before discussing in any detail the role of the nursery school, and of the teacher in particular, that this report should attempt to set down a summary of what the infant needs from the mother, and the nature of the role that the mother plays in fostering healthy psychological development in the child's earliest years. It is only in the light of the mother's role and the child's needs that a real understanding can be gained of the way in which the nursery school can continue the mother's work.

Any statement of a child's need in infancy and at the nursery school age must, if it is to be brief, do gross injustice to its subject. Nevertheless, even though a fully agreed and yet detailed statement could hardly be expected at the present stage of our knowledge, the account of broad outlines that follows appears to those members of the expert group particularly concerned with the clinical study of psychological development in infancy to be one that would be generally accepted by other workers in the field.

A few preliminary remarks are necessary on the respective roles of the mother, the nursery school teacher, and the teacher of older children.

A *mother* need not have intellectual understanding of her job because she is fitted for it in its essentials by her biological orientation to her own baby. It is the fact of her devotion to her own baby rather than her self-conscious knowledge that makes her good enough to be successful in the early stages of infant nurture.

A *young nursery school teacher* is not orientated biologically to any one child, except indirectly through identification with a mother figure. It is necessary therefore for her to be brought gradually to see that there exists a complex psychology of infant growth and adaptation, with need for special environmental conditions. Discussion of the children in her care will enable her to recognise the dynamic nature of normal emotional growth.

A *senior teacher* must be more able to appreciate intellectually the nature of this problem of growth and adaptation. Fortunately, she need not know everything, but she should be temperamentally fitted to accept the dynamic nature of growth processes and the complexity of the subject, and eager to increase her knowledge of detail by objective observations and by planned studies. She can be greatly helped by having opportunity for discussion of *theory* with child psychologists, psychiatrists, and psycho-analysts, and, of course, by reading.

The role of the father is vitally important, at first through his material and emotional support of his wife, and then gradually through his direct relation to his infant. At the nursery school age, he may have become more important to his child than the mother. Nevertheless, it is not possible to do justice to the role of the father in the statement that follows.

The nursery school years are significant because of the fact that a child at this period is in transition from one stage to another. While in some important ways and at some moments the 2–5-year-old child reaches to a maturity resembling that of the adolescent, in other ways and at other moments the same child is also (normally) immature and infantile. It is only when the mother's early care has been successful and when, in addition, the parents continue to provide the environmental essentials that the nursery school teachers can give their mothering function second place to pre-school education proper.

In practice, every child at a nursery school is at certain moments and in certain ways an infant needing mothering (and fathering).

Also to a greater or lesser extent there may have been maternal failure, and the nursery school then has the chance to supplement and correct maternal failure when this is not severe. For these reasons the young teacher needs to learn about mothering, and she has opportunity for this through her conversations with and through her observations of the mothers of the children in her care.

Normal Psychology of Childhood and Early Infancy

In the age period 2–5 or 7, each normal infant is experiencing the most intense conflicts which result from the powerful instinctual trends that enrich feelings and personal relationships. The quality of instinct has become less like that of early infancy (mainly alimentary) and more like that which is recognised later, at puberty, as the foundation of the sexual life of adults. The conscious and unconscious fantasy life of the child has taken on a new quality which makes possible identifications with mothers and fathers, wives and husbands, and the bodily accompaniments of these fantasy experiences have come to involve excitements which are like those of normal adults.

At the same time, relationships have only just become established as between whole human beings. Further, at this age, the little boy or girl is still learning to perceive external reality, and to understand that the mother has a life of her own, and that she cannot actually be possessed as she belongs to someone else.

The consequence of these developments is that ideas of love are followed by ideas of hate, by jealousy and painful emotional conflict, and by personal suffering, and where conflict is too great there follows loss of full capacity, inhibitions, 'repression',[1] etc., resulting in symptom formation. Expression of feeling is partly direct, but it is more and more possible, as the development of a child proceeds, for relief to be obtained by self-expression through play and through the medium of speech.

In these matters the nursery school has obvious important functions. One such is the provision for a few hours a day of an emotional atmosphere that is not the highly charged one of the home. This gives the child breathing-space for personal development. Also new triangular relationships less highly charged than at home can be formed and can be expressed among the children themselves.

[1] This word is used in its technical psychological sense.

16

The school, which stands for the home, but which is not an alternative to the child's home, can provide opportunity for a deep personal relationship with someone other than the child's parents. It provides this opportunity in the persons of the staff and the other children, and a generally tolerant but steady framework in which experiences can be lived through.

It is vital to remember, however, that at the same time that there are these evidences of achievement in the process of maturation, in other respects there is immaturity. For instance, the capacity for accurate perception is not fully developed, so that we expect from a small child a subjective rather than an objective conception of the world, especially at times such as those of going to sleep and waking. When anxiety threatens, the child easily returns to the infantile position of dependence, often with the consequence that infantile incontinence reappears, as well as infantile intolerance of frustration. Because of this immaturity the school has to be able to take over the function of the mother who gave the infant confidence at the beginning.

It cannot be assumed that the child of nursery school age has a fully established capacity to maintain love and hate of the same person. The more primitive way out of conflict is to split the good from the bad. The child's mother, who has inevitably stimulated in the child both love and anger, has continued to exist and to be herself, and by this she has enabled the child to begin to bring together what seems good and what seems bad in her; so the child has started to have guilt feelings, and to be concerned about the aggression that becomes directed towards her through love of her, and through her insufficiencies.

There is a fine factor involved in the development of guilt and concern. The sequence is: love (with aggressive elements), hate, a period of digestion, guilt, reparation through direct expression or through constructive play. If the opportunity for reparation is missing, then the child must react by loss of capacity for guilt feeling, and ultimately by loss of capacity to love. The nursery school continues this work of the mother by the stability of its personnel, and also by its provision for constructive play, which enables each child to discover a way of dealing with the guilt that belongs to aggressive and destructive impulses.

A very important task already performed by the mother can be described under the term 'weaning'. Weaning implies that the mother has given something good, that she has waited till signs developed that the child was ready to be weaned, and that she has carried through with the task, in spite of arousing angry responses. When the child goes from home-care to school-care this experience is to some extent reproduced, so that a study of the weaning history of a child materially helps the young teacher to understand the initial difficulties which may appear at school. When a child takes to school easily the teacher can see this as an extension of the mother's success with her task of weaning.

There are other ways in which the mother, without knowing it, performs essential tasks in the laying down of the basis for her child's subsequent mental health. For instance, without her careful presentation of external reality the child has no means of making a satisfactory relationship with the world.

In nursery school education, provision is made for that which is intermediate between the dream and the real; notably, play is respected in a positive way, and stories and drawings and music are employed. It is especially in this field that the nursery school can give enrichment and can help the child to find a working relationship between ideas that are free and behaviour that needs to become group-related.

By constantly looking for and seeing the human being in her infant, the mother has been enabling the infant gradually to come together as a personality, to integrate from within into a unit. This process is not completed by nursery school age, and during this period the need continues for a personal type of relationship, with each child known by name, and dressed and treated according to what that child is and feels like. In the favourable case, the individuality of the child becomes in the course of time so firm that it is the child who wants to join in group activities.

The *physical* care of the infant from birth (or before) onwards has been a *psychological* process from the child's point of view. The mother's technique of holding, of bathing, of feeding, everything she did to the baby, added up to the child's first idea of the mother, and to this there was gradually added her looks and her other physical attributes and her feelings.

The child's ability to feel that the body is the place where the psyche lives could not have developed without a consistent technique of handling, and when the nursery school continues with the provision of a physical environment and with the bodily care of the children, it is performing a main task of *mental* hygiene. Feeding is never simply a matter of getting food in; it is another way in which the school teacher continues the work of the mother. The school, like the mother, shows love by feeding the child, and, like the mother, expects to be refused (hated, suspected) as well as accepted (trusted). In the nursery school there is no place for what is impersonal or mechanical, because, for the child, this means hostility or (worse still) indifference.

The picture of the mother's role and the child's needs set out in this section makes it clear that the nursery school teacher needs to be in touch with maternal functions, and this is consistent with the fact that her main task concerns the educational functions of the primary school. There is a lack of teachers of psychology, but everywhere there is a source of information which can be tapped by the nursery school teacher if she be so directed : the observation of infant care by mothers and fathers, in the family setting.

THE ROLE OF THE NURSERY SCHOOL TEACHER

On the assumption that the nursery school supplements and extends in certain directions the function of the good home, the nursery school teacher naturally takes over some of the attributes and duties of the mother for the school period, without however seeking out of her own needs to develop a maternal emotional bond. Her duty is rather to maintain, strengthen, and enrich the child's personal relationship with the family, at the same time introducing a wider world of people and opportunities. Thus, from the time of the child's first entry into school a sincere and cordial relationship between the teacher and the mother will serve to arouse a sense of confidence in the mother and reassurance in the child. The establishment of such a relationship will help the teacher to detect and understand those disturbances in her children that arise from circumstances in the home, and in many cases it will afford opportunities to the teacher for helping mothers to have greater faith in themselves as mothers.

The entry into a nursery school is a social experience outside the family. It creates a psychological problem for the child and an opportunity for the nursery teacher to make her first mental hygiene contribution.

The entry into the school may also create anxieties for the mother, who may misinterpret the child's need for the opportunities for development beyond the scope of the home, and who may feel that this need arises from her own inadequacy rather than from the child's natural development.

These problems, which arise on the child's entry into the nursery school, exemplify the fact that throughout the whole period at the nursery school the teacher has a dual responsibility, and a dual opportunity. She has the opportunity of assisting the mother to discover her own maternal potentialities, and of assisting the child in working through the inevitable psychological problems which face the developing human being.

Loyalty to the home and respect for the family are fundamental in the maintenance of firm relationships between the child, the teacher, and the family.

The teacher assumes the role of a warm-hearted and sympathetic friend, who will not only be the mainstay of the children's life away from home but also a person resolute and consistent in her behaviour towards them, discerning of their personal joys and sorrows, tolerant of their inconsistencies, and able to help them at times of special need. Her opportunities lie in her personal relationship with the child, with the mother, and with all the children as a group. She has, in contrast to the mother, technical knowledge derived from her training, and an attitude of objectivity towards the children under her care.

Apart from the teacher and her relationship with individual children, their mothers, and the children as a group, the nursery school setting as a whole makes important contributions to the child's psychological development. It provides a physical setting more appropriate to the level of the child's capacities than the home in which the furniture is scaled to the giant size of adults, in which space is compressed by size of modern dwellings, and in which those around the child are inevitably more concerned with the task of keeping the domestic wheels turning than with creating a situation in which the child can develop new capacities through play—a creative activity which is essential for every child's development.

The nursery school also provides the child with the companionship of others of the same age. It is the child's first experience of being one of a group of equals, and so faces him with the need to develop the capacity for harmonious relationships in such a group.

In their early years, children are undertaking simultaneously three psychological tasks. First, they are building a conception of themselves as a 'self' with a relationship to reality as they begin to conceive it. Second, they are developing a capacity for a relationship with a person, the mother. The mother has enabled the child to develop in these two respects to a considerable extent before going to the nursery school and indeed, at first, the entry into the school is a shock to the personal relationship with the mother. The child faces this shock by developing another capacity, namely the capacity for a personal relationship with someone other than the mother. It is because the nursery teacher is the object of this personal relationship apart from the mother that she must recognise that for the child she is not an 'ordinary' person and cannot behave in an 'ordinary' way. She must, for instance, accept the idea that the child can only gradually come to share her without getting upset.

The capacity to share her will grow as the child successfully makes a third type of development, namely that of the capacity for relationships in which several people are involved. How far any one child will have developed in these three respects by the time of nursery school age will depend very largely on the nature of that child's previous experience with the mother. The three processes of development will continue side by side.

The process of development, as it continues, creates 'normal' problems which manifest themselves frequently at the nursery school in the child's behaviour. Although the occurrence of such problems is normal and frequent, the child needs help in solving them, for failure here may leave its mark on the child's personality throughout life.

Because young children of pre-school age tend to be the victims of their own strong emotions and aggressiveness, the teacher must at times protect the children from themselves and exert the control and guidance necessary in the immediate situation, and, in addition, ensure the proper provision of satisfying activities in play to help the children to guide their own aggressiveness into constructive channels and to acquire effective skills.

Throughout the whole of this period, there is a two-way process between the home and the school, stresses arising in the one *milieu* being manifested as disturbances of behaviour in the other. When the child's behaviour is disturbed at home, the teacher can often help the mother to understand what is happening from her experience of the child's problems at school.

Through her knowledge of the normal phases of growth, she must also be prepared for sudden and dramatic changes in behaviour and learn to tolerate jealous feelings arising from disturbances in the family setting. Breakdowns in cleanliness, difficulties in feeding and sleeping, retardation in speech, faulty motor activity, these and other symptoms may present themselves as normal problems of growth or, in an exaggerated form, as deviations from the normal.

She will also be faced in the child's early period at the school with a bewildering fluctuation between moods of great dependence and independence; also, even towards the end of the nursery school age, a confusion between right and wrong, between fantasy and fact, between what is personal property and what belongs to others.

The teacher needs enough knowledge to guide her to the appropriate treatment, either within the nursery school or else by referring to a specialist.

Upon the organisation and provision of occupations and activities in the nursery school depends the full flowering of the emotional, social, intellectual, and physical potentialities of the child. The teacher plays an essential role in these activities in combining a sensitivity to and knowledge of children's symbolic language and expression, and an appreciation of the special needs of children within a group. Furthermore, ingenuity and resourcefulness in providing the necessary equipment must be combined with understanding of the value in different forms of play, e.g. dramatic, creative, free, organised, constructional, etc.

In the pre-school years play is the child's principal means of solving the emotional problems that belong to development. Play is also one of the child's methods of expression—a way of telling and asking. The teacher needs an intuitive realisation of this if she is to help the child with the painful problems which inevitably exist, of which adults are often so unaware, and she needs training which will help her to develop and use this realisation of the significance of play to the pre-school child.

Education in the nursery school demands that the teacher shall be ready to exert restraints and controls over such impulses and instinctual desires, common to all children, as are unacceptable in their own communities, at the same time providing the tools and opportunities for the full creative and intellectual development of young children, and the means of expression for their fantasy and dramatic life.

And, finally, inseparable from her work with children, is the teacher's capacity to work in harmony with other members of the staff and to preserve in herself her womanly qualities.

23

On Influencing and Being Influenced

[1941]

N o doubt the great stumbling-block in scientific enquiry into human affairs has been the difficulty man has found in recognising the existence and importance of feelings that are unconscious. Of course people have long shown that they knew of the unconscious; they knew what it was like, for instance, to feel an idea come and go, to recover a lost memory, or to be able to call on inspiration, whether benign or malignant. But there is a very great difference between such intuitive flashes of recognition of fact, and the intellectual appreciation of the unconscious and its place in the scheme of things. Great courage was needed for this discovery of unconscious feelings, a discovery which will always be linked with the name of Freud.

Courage was needed, because, once we accept the unconscious, we are on a path which sooner or later takes us to something very painful—the recognition that however much we try to see evil, beastliness, and bad influence as something outside ourselves, or impinging on us from without, in the end we find that whatever things people do and whatever influences actuate them, these are in human nature itself, in fact, in *ourselves*. There certainly can be such a thing as a harmful environment, but (provided we have made a good start) the difficulties we find in coping with such an environment come chiefly from the fact of the existence of essential conflicts within. This, again, man has long known in intuitive flashes; one might say ever since the first human being committed suicide.

Nor does man find it easy to accept as coming from his own

nature the good influences and the things he attributes to God.

Our power to think things out about human nature, then, is liable to be blocked by our fear of the full implication of what we find.

Against a background of recognition of the unconscious as well as of the conscious in human nature, one can study details of human relationships with profit. One aspect of this huge subject is indicated by the words : Influencing and Being Influenced.

A study of the place of influence in human relationship has always been of great importance to the teacher, and it has a special interest for the student of social life and of modern politics. This study involves us in a consideration of feelings which are more or less unconscious.

There is one kind of human relationship an understanding of which will help in the elucidation of some of the problems of influence. This kind of human relationship has roots in the early days of the individual's life, when one of the chief contacts with another human being was at feeding-time. Parallel with the ordinary physiological feeding there is a taking in, digesting, retaining, and rejecting, of the things and people and events in the child's environment. Although the child grows up and becomes able to develop other kinds of relationship, this early one persists throughout life to a greater or lesser degree, and in our language we find many a word or phrase which can be used to describe a relationship to food, or equally well to people and inedible things. With this in mind we can look at the problem we are studying, and perhaps see a little farther or a little more clearly.

Obviously there can be unsatisfied babies, and also there can be mothers urgently wishing, and wishing in vain, to have their food accepted, and it is possible to describe people who are similarly unsatisfied, or who feel frustrated in their relations to other people.

For instance, there is the person who feels empty and who fears to feel empty, and who fears the extra aggressive quality which emptiness puts into his appetite. This person may, perhaps, be empty for a known reason : a good friend has died, or something valuable has been lost; or through some more subjective cause he is depressed. Such a person has a need to find a new object with which to be filled, a new person who can take the place of the one lost, or a new set of ideas or a new philosophy to replace lost ideals. It can be seen that such a person is particularly liable to be influenced. Unless he can bear with this depression or sadness or hopelessness, and wait for a spontaneous recovery, he must go and seek a new influence, or succumb to whatever powerful influence happens to turn up.

It is also easy to picture a person with a great need to give, to fill people up, to get under their skin, really to prove to himself or herself that what he or she has to give is good. There is unconscious doubt, of course, about this very thing. Such a person must be teaching, organising, effecting propaganda, getting his or her own way through influencing others to act. As a mother, such a person is liable to overfeed or otherwise to direct her children, and there is a relation between this anxious eagerness to fill and the anxious hunger I have described. There is a fear of anxious hunger in others.

No doubt the normal drive to teach is along these very lines. All of us to some extent need our work for our own mental health, the teacher no less than the doctor or nurse. The normality or abnormality in our drive is largely a matter of degree of anxiety. But, on the whole, I think pupils prefer to feel that teachers do not have this urgent need to teach, this need to teach to keep at arm's length their own personal difficulties.

Now, it can easily be imagined what happens when these extremes meet, and the frustrated giver meets the frustrated receiver. Here is one person empty and anxiously seeking a new influence, and here is another aching to get inside someone and exert influence. In the extreme case, where one person, so to speak, swallows the other whole, the result can be a rather ludicrous impersonation. Such incorporation of one person by another can account for that spurious maturity that we often meet with, or may explain how it is that a person can seem all the time to be acting. A child who is impersonating some hero or heroine may be good, but the goodness somehow seems to be unstable. Another child acts in a bad way, impersonating an admired and feared villain, and you feel the badness is not inherent, it seems compulsive, the child is acting a part. It is a common experience to find a child with an illness which is an imitation of the illness of someone who has just died, and who was dearly loved.

It will be seen that this intimate relationship between the one influencing and the other influenced is a kind of love relationship, and can easily be mistaken for the true article, especially by the persons themselves.

Between the extremes are the majority of teacher-pupil relationships. In these the teacher likes to teach, and gets reassurance out of success, but does not absolutely need success for his or her mental health : also the pupil can enjoy going for what the teacher has to offer, without being compelled by anxiety to act like the teacher, to retain everything as it was taught, or to believe everything any one teacher teaches. The teacher has to be able to tolerate being doubted or suspected, as a mother tolerates her children's varying individual food fads, and the pupil has to be able to tolerate not immediately or reliably getting what feels acceptable.

From this it follows that some of the most eager members of the teaching profession might be limited in their practical work with their pupils exactly because of their keenness, for this keenness can make them unable to tolerate the children's sifting and testing of what is offered them, or their initial reaction of rejection. In practice these are inevitable irksome things, and they cannot be avoided except by unhealthy overriding.

These same considerations apply to the way parents bring up their children ; indeed the earlier it comes in a child's life, the more serious must be the effect of the influencing and being influenced type of relationship, when it is put forward as a substitute for love.

If a woman expects to be a mother without ever meeting the child's urge to make a mess at the moment of acute desire to defecate, if she hopes never to have to cope with the problems arising out of the clash between her convenience and the child's spontaneity, we should think her to be shallow in her love. She might override her child's desires, but the result, if successful, would be considered dull ; and success of this kind easily turns to failure, since the child's unconscious protest may unexpectedly appear in the form of intractable incontinence. Is it not similar with teaching?

Good teaching demands of the teacher a toleration of the frustrations to his or her spontaneity in giving, or feeding—frustrations that may be felt acutely. The child, in learning to be civilised, naturally also feels frustrations acutely, and is helped in becoming civilised not so much by the teacher's precepts as by the teacher's own ability to bear the frustrations inherent in teaching.

The teacher's frustration does not end with the recognition that teaching is always imperfect, that mistakes are inevitably made, and that sometimes any teacher may act meanly or unfairly, or may actually do bad things. Worse to bear than all this, the teacher's best teaching will be sometimes rejected. Children will bring to the school situation doubts and suspicions that belong to their own characters and experiences, that are part and parcel of their own emotional developmental distortions; also children will always be liable to distort what they find at school, because they will be expecting to find their home environment either reproduced there or else represented by its opposite.

The teacher has to bear with these disappointments, and, in turn, the child has to bear with the moods and character difficulties and inhibitions of the teacher. Some mornings even teachers get out of bed on the wrong side.

The more we look, the more we see that if teachers and pupils are living healthily they are engaged in a mutual sacrifice of spontaneity and independence, and that is almost as important a part of education as the teaching and learning in the set subjects. At any rate, education is poor stuff, even when the subjects are well taught, if this object lesson—'give and take'—is absent, or is overridden by dominance of one personality over another.

What conclusion can be drawn from all this?

Our thinking out has led us, as thinking about education often does, to the conclusion that nothing is more misleading in the assessment of educational methods than simple academic success or failure. Success may so easily mean no more than that a child has found that the easiest way to deal with a particular teacher, or a particular subject, or with education as a whole, is by sub-servience, a holding open of the mouth with the eyes shut, or a swallowing whole without critical inspection. This is false, because it means that there is a complete denial of very real doubts and suspicions. Such a state of affairs is unsatisfactory in respect of individual development, but it is meat and drink to a dictator.

In our consideration of influence and its proper place in education, we have come to see that the prostitution of education lies in the misuse of what could almost be called the child's most sacred attribute : *doubts about self*. The dictator knows all about this, and wields power through offering a life free from doubt. How dull!

4

Educational Diagnosis

[1946]

WHAT is there that a doctor can usefully say to a teacher? Obviously he cannot teach him how to teach, and no one wants a teacher to take up a therapeutic attitude towards pupils. Pupils are not patients. At least, they are not patients in relation to the teacher while they are being taught.

When a doctor surveys the field of education, he soon finds himself asking a question: the whole of a doctor's work is based on diagnosis; what in teaching corresponds to this in medical practice?

Diagnosis is so important to a doctor that there has been a tendency in medical schools to ignore the subject of therapy, or to relegate it to a corner where it can easily be forgotten. At the height of this phase of medical education, which was reached perhaps two or three decades ago, people spoke with enthusiasm about a new phase in medical education in which therapy would be the main thing taught. We are now presented with remarkable methods of therapy: penicillin, safe surgery, immunisation against diphtheria, and so on, and the public is deluded into thinking that the practice of medicine is thereby improved, little knowing that these very improvements threaten the foundation of good medicine, which is accurate diagnosis. If an individual is ill and feverish, and is given M. & B., and clears up in a few days, he thinks he is well served, but sociologically the case is a tragedy, because the doctor is relieved of the necessity of making a diagnosis by the fact of the patient's response to the drug, blindly administered. Diagnosis on a scientific basis is the most precious part of our medical heritage, and distinguishes the medical profession from the faith healers, and the osteopaths, and all the other people we consult when we want a flashy cure.

29

The question is, what do we see when we look at the teaching profession that corresponds with this business of diagnosis? It is quite possible that I am wrong, but I feel bound to say that I can see but little in teaching that is truly equivalent to the deliberate diagnosis of doctors. In my dealings with the teaching profession I am frequently disturbed in mind by the way in which the general mass of children are educated without first being diagnosed. Obvious exceptions spring to the mind, but I think the general statement is true. At any rate, it may be useful for a doctor to show what in his opinion could be gained from something equivalent to diagnosis, if it were seriously undertaken in the teaching world.

First of all, what is already being done in this direction? There is one way in which diagnosis comes in in every school; if a child is objectionable the tendency is for that child to be got rid of, either expelled, or removed by indirect pressure. This may be good for the school, but bad for the child, and most teachers would agree that the best thing is for such children to be eliminated at the beginning, when the Committee or the Headmaster or Headmistress 'finds it unfortunately impossible to take another child at the moment'. However, it is extremely difficult for a Head to be certain that in refusing to admit doubtful cases he at the same time is not keeping out specially interesting children. If there were a scientific method available for selection of pupils, it would doubtless be used.

Scientific method is available for measuring available intelligence, the Intelligence Quotient (I.Q.). The various tests are well known and are employed on an increasing scale, though sometimes they are used as if they meant more than they can ever do. An I.Q. can be valuable at both ends of the scale. It is helpful to know by these carefully prepared tests that a child who is not doing well is able to reach an average attainment, thus showing that it is his emotional difficulties that are holding him up, if not actually a fault in the method of teaching; and it is also helpful to know that a child is so far below the average intellectually that he almost certainly has a poor brain which cannot benefit from education designed for children with good brains. In the case of mental defectives the diagnosis is usually fairly obvious before the test is made. There is general recognition that the provision of special schools for the backward, and of occupation centres for the very backward, is an essential part of any education scheme.

So far so good. Diagnosis is being made in so far as scientific method is available. However, most teachers feel that it is natural for their classes to contain both clever and less clever children, and they naturally adapt themselves to the varying needs of their pupils in so far as the classes are not too big for them to be able to do individual work. What troubles teachers is not so much the varying *intellectual* capacity of their children, as their varying *emotional* needs. Even with regard to teaching, some children thrive on having things rammed down their throats, whereas others only learn at their own pace, and in their own way, almost in secret. With regard to discipline, groups vary greatly, and no hard and fast rule works. If kindness works in one school, it fails in another : freedom, kindness, and tolerance can produce casualties, just as an atmosphere of strictness can. And then there is the question of the emotional needs of various sorts of children—the amount of reliance on the personality of the teacher, and the mature and primitive feelings that develop in the children towards the person of the teacher. All these things vary, and although the ordinary good teacher manages to sort them out, there is often a feeling that a few children have to be denied what they obviously need for the sake of the many others, who would be disturbed if the school were to be adapted to the special needs of one or two. These are very big problems that are occupying the minds of teachers day in, day out, and a doctor's suggestion is that more could be done than is being done at present along the lines of diagnosis. Perhaps the trouble is that classification is not yet properly worked out. The following suggestions might help.

In any group of children there are those whose homes are satisfactory and those whose homes are unsatisfactory. The former naturally use their homes for their emotional development. In their case the most important testing out and acting out is done at home, the parents of such children being able and willing to take responsibility. The children come to school for something to be added to their lives ; they want to learn lessons. Even if learning is irksome, they want so many hours a day of hard work which will enable them to get through examinations, which can lead to their eventually working in a job like their parents. They expect organisation of games, because this cannot be done at home, but playing in the ordinary sense of the word is something which belongs to home, and the fringe of home life. By contrast, the other children come to school for another purpose. They come with the idea that school might possibly provide what their home has failed to provide. They do not come to school to learn, but to find a home from home. This means that they seek a stable emotional situation in which they can exercise their own emotional lability, a group of which they can gradually become a part, a group that can be tested out as to its ability to withstand aggression and to tolerate aggressive ideas. How strange that these two kinds of children find themselves in the same classroom! It should surely be possible to have different types of schools, not by chance, but by planning, adapted to these extreme diagnostic groupings.

Teachers find themselves by temperament more suitable for one or other type of management. The first group of children cries out for teaching proper, with the emphasis on scholastic instruction, and it is with children living in their own satisfactory homes (or with good homes to go back to in the case of boarding-school children) that the most satisfactory teaching is done. On the other hand, with the other group of children without satisfactory homes, the need is for organised school life with suitable staffing arrangements, regular meals, supervision of clothing, management of children's moods and of their extremes of compliance and non-cooperation. The emphasis here is on *management*. In this type of work teachers should be chosen for stability of character, or because of their own satisfactory private lives, rather than because of their ability to put across arithmetic. This cannot be done except in small groups; if there are too many children in the care of one teacher, how can each child be known personally, how can provision be made for day to day changes, and how can a teacher sort out such things as maniacal outbursts, unconsciously determined, from the more conscious testing of authority? In extreme cases the step has to be taken of providing these children with an alternative to home life in the shape of a hostel, this alone giving the school a chance to do some actual teaching. In small hostels there is immense gain from the fact that, because of the smallness of the group, each child can be totally managed over a long period of time in a personal way by a small constant staff. The relation of the staff to what remains of each child's home life is in itself a tricky and time-absorbing business, which further proves the need for the avoidance of large groups in the management of these children.

A sorting out along these lines occurs naturally in private school selection, because there are all types of schools, and all types of masters and mistresses, and gradually through agencies and hearsay parents more or less sort out themselves, and the children find themselves in suitable schools. However, where day schools have to be provided by the State, the matter is quite different. The State has to act in a relatively blind way. Children have to be provided with schooling near the neighbourhood in which they live, and it is difficult to see how there can ever be enough schools in each neighbourhood for these extremes to be catered for. The State can grasp the difference between a mental defective and an intelligent child, and can take note of anti-social behaviour, but the application of anything so subtle as a sorting out of the children who have good homes from those who have not is extremely difficult. If the State attempts to sort out good from bad homes some gross errors will be made, and these errors will necessarily interfere with the especially good parents who are unconventional and who do not plan for appearances.

In spite of these difficulties, it seems to be worth while to draw attention to this sort of fact. Extremes sometimes usefully illustrate ideas. It is easy to say that a child who is anti-social and whose home has failed for one reason or another needs special management, and this can help us to see that so called 'normal' children can already be divided into those whose homes are coping, and for whom education is a welcome addition, and those who expect from their school the essential qualities lacking in their own home.

The subject is even more complex because of the fact that some of the children who could be classified with those who lack a good home actually have a good home of which they are not able to make use, because of their own personal difficulties. Many families of several children have one who is unmanageable at home. It is a justifiable simplification, however, to make a division between those children whose homes can cope with them and those whose homes cannot cope with them, for the sake of illustrating a point. It would be necessary in a further development of this theme to make a further distinction between those children whose homes have failed them after making a good start, and those children who have had no satisfactory consistent personal introduction to the world at all, not even in early infancy. Along with these latter children will be those whose parents could have given these necessary things had not something interrupted the process, such as an operation, a long stay in hospital, a mother having suddenly to leave the child because of illness, and so on.

In a few words I have tried to show that teaching could very well base itself, as good medical practice does, on diagnosis. I have chosen only one kind of classification in order to make my meaning clear. This does not mean that there are not other and perhaps more important ways of sorting children. Sorting according to age and according to sex has certainly been much discussed among teachers. Further sorting could usefully be done according to psychiatric types. How strange to teach withdrawn and preoccupied children along with the extraverted and those whose goods are in the shop window! How strange to give the same teaching to a child in a depressive phase as is given to that child when the phase has given way to a more care-free mood! How strange to have one technique for the harnessing of true excitement and for the management of the ephemeral and unstable contra-depressive swing, or elated mood!

Of course, teachers do intuitively adapt themselves and their methods of teaching to the various and varying conditions that they meet with. In a sense this idea of classification and diagnosis is already even stale. Yet the suggestion is made here that teaching should be officially based on diagnosis, just as good medical practice is, and that intuitive understanding on the part of the specially talented teachers is not good enough for the profession as a whole. This is particularly important in view of the spread of State planning, which tends always to interfere with the talents of individuals, and to produce quantitative increase of accepted theory and practice.

5

Shyness and Nervous Disorders
in Children

[1938]

I T is the doctor's business to attend, for the moment at least, to
the individual needs of one patient—the patient brought to him
for consultation. A doctor, therefore, is perhaps not the right
person to talk to teachers, since teachers practically never have the
opportunity to confine their attentions to one child at a time. Often
they must feel a desire to do what would seem excellent for one
child, and yet refrain for fear of causing a disturbance in the
group as a whole.

This is not to say, however, that the teacher has no interest in
a study of the individual children in his care, and what a doctor
can say may possibly cause him to see a little more clearly what
is happening when, for instance, a child is shy, or phobic. Increased
understanding can lead to lessened anxiety and better management,
even when little direct advice can be given.

There is one thing a doctor does that might be done more than
it is by teachers. The doctor gets from the parents as clear a picture
as he can of the child's past life, and of his present state, and he
tries to relate the symptoms for which the child is brought to the
child's personality, and to his external and internal experiences. The
teacher has not always enough time or has not full opportunity for
this, but I would suggest that what opportunity does present itself
for diagnosis is not always used. Often the teacher may know what
a child's parents are like, especially when they are 'impossible', over-
fussy, or neglectful; and the position in the family can be learned.
But there is so much more.

35

Even if the internal development be ignored, a great deal can often be attached to such events as the death of a favourite brother or sister, aunt or grandparent, or, of course, to the loss of one of the parents themselves. I may see a child who was managing quite normally until, say, a big brother was run over and killed, but who since that date has been liable to be morose, to have pains in the limbs, to be sleepless, to find schooling irksome, to make friends only with difficulty. I may easily find that no one has troubled to seek out these facts or to string them together, and the parents who have all the facts at their command have had at the same time to deal with their own grief, and so are liable to have been unconscious of the connection between the change in the child's state and the family's loss.

The consequence of such a lack of history-taking is that the teacher joins with the school doctor in a set of mistakes in management that can only confuse the child, who longs for someone to bring understanding.

Of course, the ætiology of most of the children's nervousness and shyness is not as simple as this; more often than not, there is no clear precipitating external factor, but the teacher's method should be such that, if such a factor exists, it cannot be missed.

I always remember a very simple case of this kind—that of an intelligent girl of 12 who had become nervous at school and enuretic at night. No one seemed to have realised that she was struggling with her grief at her favourite brother's death. This little brother had gone away supposedly for a week or two with an infectious fever, but he had not come home immediately as he developed a pain that turned out to be due to a tuberculous hip. The sister had been glad with the rest of the family that he was placed in a good tuberculosis hospital. In the course of time he suffered much more pain, and when at last he died of generalised tuberculosis, she had been glad again. It was a happy release, they had all said.

Events had taken place in such a way that she never experienced acute grief, and yet grief was there, waiting for acknowledgment. I caught her with an unexpected 'You were very fond of him, weren't you?' which produced loss of control, and floods of tears. The result of this was a return to normal at school, and a cessation of the enuresis at night.

Such an opportunity for direct therapy does not turn up every day, but the case illustrates the helplessness of the teacher and doctor who do not know how to take an accurate history.

Sometimes diagnosis becomes clear only after a good deal of investigation. A girl of 10 years was in a school where a good deal of trouble was taken over individuals. I saw her teacher, who said, 'This child is nervous and shy, just like so many others. I was painfully shy myself as a child, and I understand nervousness. In my class I find I can usually manage the nervous children, so that within a few weeks they lose a good deal of their shyness. But this child beats me : she seems quite unchanged by anything I can do ; she gets neither better nor worse.'

It happened that this child was treated by psycho-analysis, and the shyness did not leave her until a hidden suspicion had been unveiled and analysed : a severe psychotic illness which could not have cleared up except through analysis. The teacher was right in pointing out the difference between this shy child and others who superficially resembled her. All kindness was a trap for this child, and all gifts were poisoned apples. She could neither learn nor feel secure while she was ill, and she was driven by fear, too, to appear like the other children as far as she was able, so as not to give herself away as needing the help which she had no hope of receiving or accepting. After this child had been treated for a year or so, the same teacher became able to manage her just as she was able to manage the others, and eventually a girl emerged who was a credit to the school.

Many of the children who are excessively nervy have in their psychological make-up an expectation of persecution, and it is helpful to be able to distinguish these from other children. Such children often get persecuted ; they practically ask to be bullied— one could almost say that at times they produce bullies among their companions. They do not easily make friends, though they may achieve certain alliances against a common foe.

These children are brought to us with various pains and appetite disorders, but what will interest you is that they often complain that their teacher has hit them.

Fortunately we know that the object of this complaint is not the statement of God's truth. Its object is a much more complex affair, often a delusion pure and simple, sometimes a subtle misstatement, always a signal of distress, a signal of much worse unconscious persecutions, hidden, and so the more terrifying to the child. Of course, there are bad teachers, and there are teachers who hit children spitefully, but it is very seldom that one comes across these by this method. The child's complaint is nearly always a symptom of psychological illness of a persecutory type in the child.

Many children will solve their own delusion-of-persecution problems by continually doing minor wickednesses, thus producing a real persecuting teacher, who constantly punishes. The teacher is forced to strictness by such a child, and one such child in a group may enforce a strict management of the whole group, which is really only 'good' for one child. It may be helpful at times to hand such a child over to some unsuspecting colleague, and so preserve the possibility of sane treatment of the other, saner pupils.

It is, of course, wise to remember that nervousness and shyness have a healthy, normal aspect. In my department I can recognise certain types of psychological disorder by an *absence* of normal shyness. A child will hang round while I am examining another patient, and come straight to me without knowing me, and climb on to my knee. The more normal children are afraid, they make demands of me in the way of technique of reassurance. They even openly prefer their own daddy, and say so.

This normal nervousness is more obviously seen in the case of the toddler. A little child who cannot be made to fear the London streets, or even a thunderstorm, is ill. There are fearful things inside such a child, as there are inside others, but he cannot risk finding them outside, cannot let his imagination run away with him. Parents and teachers who themselves employ the flight to reality as a main defence against the intangible, grotesque, and fantastic, are sometimes deceived into thinking that a child who is not afraid of 'dogs, doctors, and black men' is just sensible and brave. But really the little child should be able to be afraid, to get relief from inside badness by seeing badness in outside persons, things, and situations. Only gradually does reality-testing modify internal fearfulness, and for no one is this process anything like complete. Bluntly, the small child who is not afraid is either pretending, bolstering up his courage, or else he is ill. But if he is ill, and full of fears, he may be reassured, according to his power to see the *goodness* that is in him outside himself, too.

Shyness and nervousness, then, are matters for diagnosis, and for consideration in relation to the age of the child. On the principle that normal children can be taught, and that ill children waste teachers' energy and time, it is important to be able to come to a conclusion as to the normality or abnormality of the symptoms in each individual case; and I have suggested that proper use of history-taking may help in this—that is, if it is combined with a knowledge of the mechanism of the child's emotional development.

6

Sex Education in Schools

[1949]

CHILDREN cannot be classed together and described all in a bunch. Their needs vary according to their home influences, the kind of children they are, and their health. However, in a brief statement on this subject of sex education it is convenient to speak generally, and not to try to adapt the main thesis to individual requirements.

Children need three things at the same time :

(1) They need persons around them in whom they can confide simply by virtue of the fact that they are trustworthy human beings with ordinary capacity for human friendship.

(2) They need instruction in biology along with other school subjects—it is assumed that biology means the truth (in so far as it is known) about life, growth, propagation, and the relation of living organisms to environment.

(3) They need continued steady emotional surroundings in which they themselves can discover each in his or her own way the upsurging of sex in the self, and the way in which this alters, enriches, complicates, and initiates human relationships.

Quite another thing is the lecture on sex, given by a person who comes to a school, delivers a talk, and then goes away. It would seem that people with an urge to teach sex to children should be discouraged. Besides, what cannot be done by the school staff cannot be tolerated by the staff either. There is something better than knowledge about sex, and that is the discovery of it by the individual.

In boarding-schools the existence of married staff with growing families in the school surround provides a natural and favourable influence, more stimulating and instructive than many lectures. In day schools the children are able to be in touch with the growing families of relations and neighbours.

The trouble about lectures is that they bring something difficult and intimate into children's lives at moments that are chosen by chance rather than by the accumulation of need in the child.

A further disadvantage of sex talks is that they seldom give a true and complete picture. For instance, the lecturer will have some bias, such as feminism, the idea that the female is passive and the male active, a flight from sex play to mature genital sex, a false theory of mother-love that leaves out the hard features and leaves only sentimentality, and so on.

Even the best sex talks impoverish the subject, which when approached from within, by experiment and experience, has the potential of infinite wealth. But it is only in an atmosphere created by the maturity of the adults that healthy adolescents can discover in themselves the body-and-soul longing for union with body and soul. In spite of these important considerations it seems that there must be room for the real experts who make a special study of sexual function and of the presentation of this sort of knowledge. Would it not be a solution to invite the experts to talk to school staffs and to develop discussions of the subject in an organised way by the teachers? The staff would then be free to act according to their own personal way in their contacts with the children, yet with a firmer foundation of knowledge of facts.

Masturbation is a sexual by-product of great importance in all children. No talk on masturbation can cover the subject, which in any case is so personal and individual that only the private talk with a friend or confidant has value. It is no use telling children in groups that to masturbate is not harmful, because perhaps for one of the group it *is* harmful, compulsive, and a great nuisance, in fact, evidence of psychiatric illness. For the others it may be harmless, and even not any trouble at all, and it is then made complex by being referred to, with the suggestion that it might be harmful. Children do, however, value being able to talk to someone about all these things, and it should have been the mother who was free to discuss absolutely anything that the child can conceive of. If mother could not do this, then others must be available, perhaps even a psychiatric interview needs to be arranged; but the difficulties are not met by sex instruction in class. Moreover, sex instruction scares away the poetry and leaves the function and sex parts high and dry and banal.

It would be more logical to point out in the art class that ideas and imaginative flights have bodily accompaniments, and that these need to be revered, and attended to, as well as ideas.

There is one obvious difficulty for those who have adolescents in their care. It is no use whatever if those who talk about allowing and even expecting children to discover themselves and each other sexually blind themselves to the existence of the liability of some of the girls to become accidentally pregnant. This problem certainly is a real one, and has to be faced, because the illegitimate child has an unhappy position, and has a much greater task than the ordinary child if he is to make the grade and eventually become a social being; indeed unless adopted at a very early stage, the illegitimate child is unlikely to come through without scars, and perhaps ugly ones. Every one who manages adolescents must cope with this problem according to his or her own convictions, but public opinion ought to take into account the fact that in the best type of management risks are taken and accidents do occur. In free schools, where there is practically no ban on sex, the illegitimate child is surprisingly rare, and when pregnancies do occur it is usual to find that one at least of the partners is a psychiatric case. There is the child, for instance, who, unconsciously fearing and fleeing from sex play, jumps right over to a spurious sexual maturity. Many children who have had no satisfactory infantile relation to their own mothers reach to inter-personal relationships for the first time in the sexual relationship, which is therefore extremely important to them, although from the onlookers' point of view insecurely mature, because not derived gradually from the immature. If there is a big proportion of such children in a group, sexual supervision must obviously be strict, because society cannot take more than a certain number of illegitimates. On the other hand, in most groups of adolescents the majority are more or less healthy, and in that case the question has to be asked, is their management to be based on what healthy children need or on society's fear of what may happen to a few anti-social or ill members?

Adults hate to think that children ordinarily have a very strong social sense. In the same way adults hate to think that little children have early guilt feelings, and quite regularly parents implant morality where a natural morality could have developed, and would have become a stable and pro-social force.

Ordinary adolescents do not want to produce illegitimate children, and they take steps to see that this does not happen. Given opportunity, they grow in their sex play and sex relationships to the point where they realise that the having of babies is what the whole thing is leading up to. This may take them years. But ordinarily this development comes, and then these new members of human society begin to think in terms of marriage, and of the setting up of the framework in which new babies and children can be.

Sex instruction has very little to do with this natural development which each adolescent must make for himself or herself. A mature and unanxious and unmoralistic environment helps so much that it can almost be said to be necessary. Also the parents and teachers need to be able to stand the surprising antagonism adolescents may develop towards adults, especially towards those who want to help at this critical time of growth.

When the parents are not able to give what is needed, the school staff or the school itself can often do a great deal to make up for this deficiency, but by example and by personal integrity and honesty and devotion and being on the spot to answer questions, and not by organised sex instruction.

For younger children the answer is biology, the objective presentation of nature, with no bowdlerisation. At first most little children like to keep and to learn about pets and to collect and understand the ways of flowers and insects. Somewhere in the period before adolescence they can enjoy progressive instruction in the ways of animals, their adaptation to environment, and their ability to adapt environment to themselves. In amongst all this comes the propagation of the species, and the anatomy and physiology of copulation and pregnancy. The biological instructor that children value will not neglect the dynamic aspects of the relationship between the animal parents and the way family life develops in the evolutionary series. There will not be much need for conscious application of what is taught in this way to human affairs, because it will be so obvious. It is more likely that the children will by subjective elaboration see human feelings and fantasies into the affairs of animals than that they will blindly apply the so-called animal instinctual processes to the affairs of the human race. The teacher of biology, like the

43

teacher of any other subject, will need to be able to direct the pupils towards objectivity and the scientific approach, expecting this discipline to be very painful to some of the children.

The teaching of biology can be one of the most pleasant and even the most exciting of tasks for the teacher, chiefly because so many children value this introduction to the study of what life is about. (Others, of course, come at the meaning of life better through history, or the classics, or in their religious experiences.) But the application of biology to the personal life and feelings of each child is altogether another matter. It is by the delicate answer to the delicate question that the linking up of the general to the particular is done. After all, human beings are not animals; they are animals plus a wealth of fantasy, psyche, soul, or inner world potential or whatever you will. And some children come at the soul through the body and some come to the body through the soul. Active adaptation is the watchword in all child care and education.

To sum up, full and frank information on sex should be available for children, but not as a thing so much as a part of the children's relationship to known and trusted people. Education is no substitute for individual exploration and realisation. True inhibitions are resistant to education, and in the average case for which psychotherapy is not available, these inhibitions are best dealt with through the understanding of the devoted friend.

7

Pitfalls in Adoption
[1954]

THE subject of adoption is a very large one, and it cannot be
covered in a short article. Preparation for work in the field
of arranging adoptions requires a knowledge of the law,
an understanding of the emotional development of the human being
starting from a very early age, and also training in case work.
Those who are preparing to become qualified to arrange adoptions
do case work under supervision, and become familiar with the technique of the follow-through.

In actual fact, only about 30 per cent of adoptions are arranged
through the adoption societies. The rest are at present either third-
party adoptions or are direct placings by the mother or are arranged
in a more or less haphazard way. It often happens that a gynæcolo-
gist or a general practitioner meets during the same week a mother
who is unable to keep her baby and a family wishing for some
reason or other to adopt a child; what could be more natural than
for an adoption to be arranged? The child is taken into the home
and the legal part follows. It must not be denied that these haphazard adoptions often work out well, and no doubt they will continue.

It is necessary to point out that a proportion of these haphazard
adoptions fail, and the adoption societies, when they look at these
failures, can often say, and with reason, that they could have
predicted the failure; proper case work, well done by the right
persons, would have enabled certain inevitable complications to
have been foreseen. A distorted motive, for instance, can be detected,
and, above all, the adoption societies can prevent a child being given
to a neurotic woman in the erroneous belief on the part of a doctor,
or some other third party, that if only the woman had a child to

45

look after she would be well. Good case work not only prevents disasters but also organises adoptions which would otherwise not have been possible, and it must be remembered that a failed adoption is usually disastrous for the child, so much so that it would have been better for the child had the attempt not been made.

It may be asked : Is there any argument against the more professional method? The objection to the carefully arranged adoption carried through by an adoption society is that by the very fact of care being taken there is often a delay; this delay can be serious and can destroy good work. In order to make certain that a baby is healthy, observations and investigations are made, and all this takes weeks or months, so that by the time the adoptive parents have an infant in their care too much has happened already in the infant's life. In fact, there has commonly been a muddle of infant care before the infant is taken over, the result of which is that the adoptive parents find themselves landed with a psychologically complex problem as well as with an infant. Also, the emotional adjustment to the idea of adopting a baby taps very deep sources of feeling. Parents who have at last made up their minds to adopt a baby are just then ripe for the adoption, and a delay of even a few months may be unhealthy. Several postponements and a delay, perhaps of months, or even years, may make the adoption no longer good, since the parents, although still willing to do what they had intended to do, have lost that special orientation towards the care of a small baby, a special orientation which at the right moment they had acquired, in a way somewhat similar (though much less intense) to that which real parents acquire naturally towards their own baby born after nine months of waiting.

From a consideration of these few observations it will already be obvious that there is no simple rule that can be followed. The student of the subject needs to read widely, and to doctors it can be said that a light-hearted arranging of an adoption implies a lack of real understanding of the factors involved. Above all, let adoptions not be arranged for the cure of adult neurosis.

The basic underlying principle is that if a baby cannot be brought up by the real parents, then the next best thing is for that baby to be taken into a family and brought up as one of the family. Moreover, a legal adoption gives the child a sense of being one of the family. The idea that a young human being can be brought up in an institution, even a good one, and automatically turn into a mature human being by growth, has long been disproved. The internal tendency towards development and the very complex emotional growth of each baby require certain conditions, and these conditions are not to be stated in terms of good bodily care. A child needs to be loved, and there are reasons for this which can be put down in black and white. It is not that a human being can be made by the environment or by good nurture, and even by the loving care of parents, but that loving care is necessary for the innate processes of emotional growth.

Instead of attempting to collect together the joys and the pitfalls that belong to the adopting of children, I have chosen to give an ordinary case history. Like any other case history, this illustrates certain points, especially that ordinary bodily care is not enough. I give the case of a child adopted for good reasons who developed difficulties and who is coming through them. The adoption was not ideal, but it is not useful to be looking always for the ideal. The fact is that this child, if he comes through, will be very much better off than if he had been brought up in an institution from the beginning. (The details have been altered in unimportant respects so that the case is unrecognisable.)

WILLIAM, AGED 4 YEARS

The two parents brought this adopted child for consultation because of the symptom : head-banging. They have had the boy under treatment at a child guidance clinic. The mother has gained a good deal of insight through contact with a member of the staff of the clinic. The boy has attended a small group for weekly sessions. As it turned out the parents were wanting a general review of the whole subject.

The interview was a ragged one. First, I saw all three together. An attempt to see the boy alone failed, and I saw the father with the boy constantly running in. Then the father and mother changed places, and afterwards the boy stayed with me alone. Eventually I had a fairly long talk with the mother.

The picture was of a deprived child, and at first it was difficult to see how this had come about, since the boy was adopted at one month (legally at four months), through a registered adoption society.

Family History

There are no children of the marriage. It was at a late stage in the consultation that I discovered that there had been an abortion before marriage. In the marriage, sexual intercourse was satisfactory, but there was found to be an obstruction of the Fallopian tubes so that no new pregnancy is likely to occur. There has been a great deal of guilt-feeling around all this, but the parents are now well on the way to recovery from the effect of these events. The mother does not resent giving up her professional life. In order to give the feeling of a family these parents have taken in many children on a temporary basis, so there are nearly always children in the house apart from William. This has helped him considerably. Now the parents have made application for a girl, and this may materialise, but there has been a very long wait, as is usual.

Past History

Birth details unknown. Breast-fed three weeks. Bottle feeding was rapidly substituted for breast feeding in preparation for the change to occur at one month. At adoption at one month, William was small, but doing well. There was no difficulty physically during infancy and the boy has had little ill-health. He had tonsillectomy at 2 years. At first it seemed that there was no disturbance of emotional development, but it gradually became evident in the consultation that neither of the parents had a rich memory of the infancy details. At the age of 2 the boy started head-banging, and this became very severe. He would sit against the wall and bang back. Then he adopted a special chair to bang back into. There is a sequence frequently observed : first, the banging, then a terrible tenseness, and then limpness, after which the boy is tired and has rings round his eyes. This compulsive behaviour has gradually become less obvious and is represented at the present time by a jigging up and down. At 2 or 3 there appeared a sensuous element in the kissing.

While the consultation was in progress the boy was showing pictures of animals to his mother, and he seemed to have a satisfactory relationship to both parents. A restlessness was evident, however. I said to the parents : 'This head-banging represents a deprivation of some sort, and I cannot see how it came about'.

Additional Notes

William never sucked fingers or thumbs, and this was not due to his having been restrained. From 2 or earlier he has adopted objects for affectionate hugging in the usual way, but a variation on the theme of head-banging has become a technique for going to sleep. He lies and thrashes the top of his head with his arm. Usually the predominant note is a wish to do this, but the compulsive element was shown when, in a bad attack of diarrhœa and sickness, he was awake and banging badly and was restrained. He kept on saying: 'I can't stop banging', and was very unhappy. Another feature was that he has never attempted to get out of his cot. There has been an apathy about his relationship to the world. Even now in the morning he never gets out of bed on his own account. Also, in the course of free play he goes off of his own accord to the chair and rocks forward and backward. If interested in some activity, however, as he may be over short periods of time, his concentration and perseverance is normal and keen, but at the slightest frustration or hurt the constructive element is lost, the play breaks down, and despair takes the place of happiness. There is a compulsive element about his needs. There has been no stealing, except, perhaps, taking a knob of sugar or a bit of cake surreptitiously. His imagination is good, but it is difficult to disentangle this from the mother's attitude, since recently she has played with him more than a mother usually does with a child, in an effort to make up for earlier deprivation, and she has encouraged imaginative play.

The Clue to the Problem

It was only gradually that the parents came to tell me of their inability to form a good relationship to the baby when he came. The mother had had guilt about the abortion to contend with, and also her resentment that the child was not her own. The father unexpectedly felt a deep revulsion on first seeing the baby. In consequence of these matters the baby was well cared for physically, but over a period of time, perhaps a year, he was not actually loved; and there was certainly no initial specialised orientation on the part of the mother to the infant's needs corresponding to that which comes naturally when a mother has a baby of her own. These parents had not been able to love the child at first, and they had only come round to a full sense of responsibility and to a loving attitude gradually. The parents could not do anything about this in the early stages, and they hoped it would not matter, but the head-banging brought them to see that damage had been done. Fortunately, they have gradually become fond of the child, and are now doing everything possible to make up for their early lack of love; they seem to me to be truly loving and easily accessible for the child. William is intelligent, and he is affectionate, although with a certain lability of affect. He has common sense. His dependence on his mother at the present time is great. He never expresses any feelings about his mother at all, and both parents feel that this is due to the fact that the mother has had an inability to show her own feelings towards the child until quite recently.

With me alone the boy drew with grand, impulsive gestures. He was able to tell me what he was drawing and to see the funny side of it. Each drawing he took to show his mother. His drawings showed his capacity for impulsive action which is becoming harnessed to the process of self-expression. He showed imagination and a sense of humour, and a certain amount of capacity to guy his own idiosyncrasies. He enjoyed the contact with me and also was willing to leave. In these respects he showed that there is much that is normal for his age in his personality development.

COMMENT

The adoption of this baby was arranged at a suitably early date. Case work was deficient in that the difficulties that the parents would experience were not predicted. One can say that if better adoptive parents had been available the child would not have developed illness; nevertheless, it is not at all certain that better parents would have been available, and the child can still count himself lucky that he was not left to more impersonal care. There happened to be factors belonging to the parents' personal life which made it impossible for either of them to feel *love* towards the infant at the beginning. They hoped to get away with it by giving specially good *physical* care, and at that time they had not sufficient insight to understand what they were doing, nor had they enough freedom from sense of personal failure to give themselves to a study of the problems associated with adopting an infant. By the time the child had begun to develop symptoms they had come round to being fond of him, and with a certain amount of help they were able at last to apply themselves seriously to the task which they had undertaken. They now have a 'case' on their hands, and they are being forced to exaggerate this and that aspect of child care in order to meet the boy's needs, that is to say, they are doing psychotherapy as well as enjoying the upbringing of a child. It happens that they are glad to have the opportunity to do something towards correcting the effects of their own earlier deficiency. They are succeeding in their double task, and although at the present time it is still possible to say that this boy is more liable than a normal child to develop an anti-social character, nevertheless, if the parents persevere, as they seem likely to do, they stand a good chance of having a son who will eventually contribute to their happiness. I would personally be in favour of their being now given a girl child for adoption.

An important fact in this case is the stability of the marriage of the adoptive parents, and in retrospect one can say that the degree to which they were upset at their own failure to produce a child is to some extent a measure of their own health.

In this work the ideal is not what is being sought. Any method that gives a deprived child a real and permanent home is to be welcomed. Nevertheless, in the long run it is the trained case worker who avoids the pitfalls, and who arranges the adoptions that are successful.

8

Two Adopted Children

[1953]

MANY of my readers will be acquainted with the practical problems involved in the arrangement of adoptions, in a way that I myself can never hope to be. On the other hand, because of the nature of my work, covering as it does two decades of psycho-analytic as well as paediatric practice, I have an understanding on the theoretical side which is particularly my own. I am not going to attempt a wide survey on the subject of emotional development, which comprises such things as the finding of the self, the gradual maturation of each individual, and the changes in the way in which the external factor is important, leading up to socialisation, and covering the vast area of human nature itself. Nor am I going to attempt to teach theory detail.

It is sometimes difficult, perhaps for legal reasons, to do follow-up work on adoption, but in this respect my position as a physician in private practice, and physician to what used to be called a voluntary hospital, has given me many opportunities for being consulted over long periods by parents who have adopted children. I intend to draw on this kind of experience and to do very little more than to describe two children, Peter and Margaret, adopted into a family. Nevertheless I would emphasise that theory is always there in the background enabling me to evaluate what I or the parents have done intuitively, and to keep a sense of proportion, and also to use that wonderful therapeutic to which attention is drawn in our saying that 'time is the great healer'. I should mention that both parents had studied psychology and had had personal analysis.

Before starting to give this human story, I wish to give you a few

---

¹ This article is based on a talk given to the Association of Child Care Officers (S.E. Area), December 5, 1953.

pointers, and I will make a brief theoretical summary at the end.

First, if an adoption goes well, then the story is an ordinary human one, and we must be familiar with the upsets and setbacks of the ordinary human story in its infinite variations if we are to understand the problems that specially belong to adoption.

The second pointer is that, even if an adoption is successful, there is something different from usual (and I think there always must be) both for the parents and for the child. For instance, for children there is an alteration in the sense of obligation, and this can cause difficulties even at a late date. Children do not have to thank their own parents for their conception although indeed they can blame them. They can take it that their parents experienced something very valuable to themselves in all that led up to the point at which conception occurred. With adopted children it is otherwise. You can put it in many different ways, but the fact remains that the parents who conceived them are unknown and unattainable, and to their adoptive parents their actual relationship cannot reach to the most primitive levels of their capacity for relationship. In some cases where there are troubles, this becomes so important a feature that adopted children when they grow up make it their business to do research into the subject of their own origin, and are not contented until they eventually find one or both of their real parents. This point does not emerge in the case of the two children I am going to describe, but then I am able to give only the surface phenomena. Both children are now grown-up and doing well, but if we had an intimate knowledge of either it is probable that we should find problems left over. The following extract from a letter to the adoptive mother from one of Margaret's closest friends is of interest in this connection :

'I cannot remember one single time when Margaret spoke unhappily or bitterly or puzzledly about being adopted . . . I do not think Margaret has "worried" about being adopted—as such—but during the last six years or so she has worried about things and been unhappy over some, as all adolescent females do, and the fact that she was adopted may have made her more sensitive . . . she belongs to you and Frank so irrevocably that she is, *I think,* completely incurious about the adoption part of it. Of all the people I know who are adopted, I think Margaret is the one who gives the strongest impression of not being so, that is to say, of not being conscious of it. I know we are both infuriating creatures at times . . . we both brood over the iniquities of our parents! but fundamentally they don't really worry us.'

The third point comes out rather clearly, which is that a very great deal depends on the history of the infant prior to adoption. I am so impressed with this point that I feel extremely critical of legislation and adoptive habits which involve delay; moreover I think that when the early days and weeks of infancy have been muddled, an infant must necessarily be a burden, and adoptive parents should be fully informed. This explains why it is that adoptions arranged in an unskilled way (by doctors, for instance) often prove successful. I have dabbled in this myself. The point is that whereas parents accept naturally the burdens that result from their own relative failure in the early management of their children (and relative failure there must often be), do they so easily accept failures that are not their own, and tolerate the burdens which belong to environmental failure previous to the adoption and for which they cannot feel themselves to be responsible?

In the cases of the two children I am describing you will see that the first child, Peter, had a good start, and most of the difficulties met with in his management were ordinary human problems. The second child, Margaret, had a bad start, and the difficulties encountered were very much of the type that could have been predicted at the time of adoption.

I am therefore dividing adoption problems into two broad categories; in one are those problems that belong quite simply to the fact of adoption and are present, although they may not give rise to anxiety; in the other are the complications that result from the defective management of the infant prior to adoption. The former we can talk about in a general way and the broad principles apply to all cases. In regard to the latter, there is obviously a wide variation according to the case. By a study of the early history, if we know it, we can predict to foster-parents how much difficulty they will have to meet and the nature of the management problems which they will encounter. If when arranging an adoption we know the early history of the infant and the degree of environmental muddle which must have essentially complicated the very early stages of the child's emotional development, we are in a position to see in advance how far the adoptive parents will be called upon

54

to provide treatment rather than ordinary child care. The problems here link up very much with the psychology of the deprived child, and when the early history has not been good enough in respect of environmental simplicity, the foster-mother is taking on not a child but a case, and in becoming a mother she becomes a therapist of a deprived child. She may succeed because the therapy she is giving is exactly the therapy that the child needs, but all along the line what she does as a mother and what the father does as a father, and what the two do together, will need to be done more deliberately, more with knowledge of what is being done, and repeatedly instead of once, on account of the fact that therapy has crept in as a complication of ordinary good management.

A further point is the obvious one that owing to the fact that adoption so easily has to be a therapy in the sense that I have described, it is even more important that adoptive parents see their children right through, than that ordinary parents do. What I mean is that whereas the ordinary child is very much enriched by the experience of being seen through to adult status by his or her own home, with the adopted child one has to say that if the home breaks up for any cause it is not so much a matter of failure of enrichment as a matter of failure of therapy, and the result is likely to be illness in the child, especially an organisation on anti-social lines.

The main purpose of what I am now going to tell you is to remind you, although you need no such reminder, that when you plant a child on parents it is not just a question of a nice little distraction for them. You are altering their whole lives. If all goes well, they will spend the next twenty-five years solving the puzzle you have set them. Of course if things do not go well, and very often they must go badly, then you are involving them in the difficult task of disappointment and the toleration of failure.

In the case of the two children Peter and Margaret, all did go well in the end, which means up to now.

PETER

In 1927, in the early days of legal adoption, a woman went to an Adoption Society to choose a child. This woman, who as a child had always had a big family of dolls, was now a teacher by profession, cultured and intelligent. When 40 she had married a lawyer,

E

a man of exceptional ability, highly cultured, several years younger than herself, of slight build. At 48 years of age, having had none of her own, she decided to adopt one or two children.

At the adoption home she immediately chose one, a boy baby who was outstandingly healthy and likeable; but this baby, although illegitimate, was not available since he belonged to a woman worker in the home who personally cared for him and breast-fed him. Disappointed, the woman went away without any baby, but after a short while the mother of the chosen baby realised her incapacity for giving the boy a good home, and arrangements were made for his adoption by these same people. The boy was said to be exceptionally strong. His putative father was a commercial traveller of very fine physique. The child was ten months when adopted, and immediately settled in and developed quite naturally, except that he was unusually powerful.

His progress was interrupted when he was just over 2 years by the fact that his father had pneumonia and his mother had 'flu. The local doctor said the boy must go away because of the risk of infection, and at first he went to friends near home. This was satisfactory, but he had to be moved to an aunt, where he proved tiresome, so he was sent to a welfare nurse whom he knew. He was happy with her, but in the middle of a meal he would stop eating, tears would roll down his cheeks, and he would say, 'Where's gone?' (Note that the word mummy had become extinguished.) When his mother eventually went to fetch him he saw her but did not go to her, so she took him and made no demands on him; he simply put his head on her shoulder and wept. At home he showed in indirect ways what he had been through. He heard a lamb bleat, and the mother said, 'The lamb has lost his mummy but will soon find her.' He said, 'I didn't cry.'

I give all this to show how healthy was this child and also his adoptive environment.

In the course of time, when he was 8 years old, Peter was sent away to school. He was growing up to be a strong youngster, reserved, and economical in show of affection. He found it difficult to return to school each term and declined to be visited there.

He never enjoyed games, and as he grew up he spent his time in the engineering shop, and on the school farm. The parents long wondered which would be the stronger—Peter's bent for mechanical things, or for animals and anything growing. He had no friends and disliked having visitors during the holidays. At school he was considered to present a problem. His writing was uniformly untidy, although school work done at home was passable. The result of his Intelligence Quotient done at school was 115, but that done more carefully at the National Institute of Industrial Psychology was consistently 138. The school reported occasional over-confidence and said that he generally combined care and decision in a very satisfactory way, also that he was level-headed, self-possessed, with a sense of humour. He had tremendous interest in, and energy for, his hobbies. He showed no interest in girls at this co-educational school.

At 16 he came to me because of difficulties at school and bad handwriting. At this age he was at his most powerful, and the parents had to accept the fact that this highly intelligent boy must not be put to academic work. I could see that this boy's wish to be an engine driver was something that could not be diverted into an engineering career, which means office work and drawing-boards. He could easily fear his own strength.

When he left school, after just managing School Certificate, the parents, strengthened by my advice, allowed him to become a mechanic. He was apprenticed to the railway workshops and at first was bored doing work he had already done at school. I was especially keen that he should come under the personal care of a man stronger than himself. Following a letter from myself, the boy was moved to the machine shop at an earlier date than he could otherwise have expected, and immediately made progress. At this time he lived with a retired foreman, and the two together did all the housework and cooking, and were devoted to each other. I think this was an important feature at this stage. We all agreed that the boy needed to plan his own life, even to details, but he needed the support that can come only from those who have a wider knowledge of affairs. Soon he had acquired a motor cycle and was coming home for the weekends. Later he came home every night, and at that time his garden was his great hobby.

After some years he moved to a more important engineering firm in the midlands, where he worked in the research workshops. Here he met the girl he has since married. He said nothing of this at home, but his mother suspected that something was up, because he came home less often. One day, being a man of few words, he asked in an indirect way whether he might bring his girl friend home. The girl had had an unhappy childhood in the care of an aunt whom she did not like, and therefore the wedding was to be from Peter's home. He wanted 'no church, no fuss, just like any ordinary day or I'll be miserable'. And so, with the minimum of ceremony, this son of a well-known and respected lawyer was married in the registry office, with no one present except the witnesses. The newly-married couple wrote, 'Thank you for a very pleasant weekend' and started their honeymoon a week later.

They now live in a caravan, the money for which Peter borrowed from his parents, but meticulously repaid. He is superintending the building of his own house. There is a baby girl aged 2 years, and Peter's attitude to her is rather curious. He says 'I'll bring her up tough. I was too much looked after when I was small.' It is not known where he got this idea from unless it can be said that his mother was over-anxious and sometimes frustrating. As a child he was affectionate till he went to school. His mother gave up kissing him at this point because it was obvious he did not want it. He never said 'thank you', and this had to be tolerated, but now he is married all this has changed, and he is even openly grateful and writes long letters home.

So here now we have a strong man of 26, husband and father and qualified engineer, very much in charge of his own affairs.

You have wondered when this boy was told that he was adopted. I think it was when he was about 3. He had asked and been told about babies. Mother said, 'You know, you came from someone else's inside, not mine. I took you over because your real mother couldn't look after you.' He seemed to accept this easily, and a few days later, seeing a Mona Lisa copy on the wall he said, 'Was that the lady I was carried in?' (His oral expression was always good.) After a few days he tried hard to make his adoptive mother say that he came out of her inside, but apart from this he has never referred to his adoption. Both parents are sure of this.

In between the two adoptions, the mother did some work for the Adoption Society, interviewing parents and watching two placings. She formed the personal opinion that parents who wanted two or more children were more deeply suitable for adopting than those who had the idea of adopting only one. Care was being taken at that time to get the right *class* of child for the adoptive parents. Nevertheless, in the case of Peter the social class discrepancy did not lead to disaster, because the boy was healthy in terms of emotional development, and because of the tolerance of the parents, who accepted not only him but also his choice of wife from the workers in the engineering shop.

Five years after adopting Peter, these same parents adopted Margaret, a baby of eleven months. Peter was only very superficially jealous, and was openly pleased. When told that she was delicate he said, 'All the more reason to keep her.'

Margaret was very different from Peter. I do not know how far it is generally recognised that a child can be a very disturbed person by eleven months, but Margaret was moderately disturbed. She was $4\frac{1}{2}$lb. at birth, and perhaps there had been attempts to get rid of her by drugs. The legal father and the putative father were both Petty Officers. The mother had no money. The baby had been somewhat starved and had had pneumonia. When adopted she was delicate and timid, and highly sensitive to noise. She wouldn't crawl. She needed a great deal of attention, and indeed she has all along been a year or two behind her age in physical and emotional development.

A great deal about Margaret's early management must be taken for granted, but I think it important that the first years of her life were dominated by one thing, the treatment for 'lazy-eye'. At eighteen months she evidently had an external squint and had glasses. An excellent orthoptist was found, and the mother went at the care of the squint as if nothing else mattered. I think this was probably the basis of the child's subsequent recovery from what might otherwise have been a permanent defect of personality, based on neglect at the early stages. In terms of the eye defect, the mother cured the personality defect. In the treatment of squint, as is well known, there is an apparatus into which the child looks and sees a cage with one eye, and a bird with the other. Trying this with her mother, Margaret would say that the bird was in the cage in order to please her. She did this same exercise in the consultation room, and the orthoptist had a way of telling that the child was fibbing. The mother felt that Margaret learned the truth in this situation with the orthoptist, and there was a moment of change which was significant when she saw the bird in the cage for the first time. This cure of the eyes was curing something in the child's personality, and a period of lying and deception and shyness in the treatment preceded the cure. As the mother remarked, 'The child learned truth from the orthoptist'. This seeing with two eyes at once was the first victory. The struggle of the mother as therapist of this child happened to take this form. The mother and child had thus had a very close relationship on a job. Special care of the eyes started at eighteen months, and from 5–7 years Margaret had intensive eye-training twice a day. The special care of the eyes lasted till the child was 13 when she was pronounced cured, and her glasses could be discarded. When she went to boarding-school she was in the middle of her treatment, and this was a cause of trouble and made Margaret disliked by the matron, who was not interested in her treatment.

The home was in the bombed area, and there had to be many moves from one day school to another during the war. Margaret was evacuated later to a safe place as a boarder, and one day she said to her mother, 'You know, you oughtn't to have done it', referring to the evacuation. But of course parents could not help being unkind at that time.

At home she began to present problems as she grew older. On one occasion she stole thirty shillings from her mother, and she had ideas that children were plotting to steal her things. She began to develop a wish that plenty of money should be available, and she still feels she is a child deprived of wealth. She worried because her parents were older than those of her many friends, and the parents kept this idea conscious in her mind.

I came into the picture when Margaret was 10, and I saw her several times in personal interview. At that time she was markedly paranoid, and what I found was the expression in 10-year-old terms of the sensitivity to noise and timidity that had been a feature even when the child was eleven months old. She blushed if she thought she was being looked at; she was shy; she had vague fears at meal times; she always had a grievance—at school she felt that the teachers were ill-tempered and overworked; she had a fear of double-decker buses; and so on. She had no zest for food, or, shall I say, she had a suspicion of food. There was compulsive masturbation. At home she maintained three constant friendships, but at boarding-school, though she craved for a bosom friend, whenever she found one there was always something undesirable.

She had been told about being adopted. At school she quickly became a disturber, even during her first days and weeks. Her friends were younger than herself. At home she must have the last word; she nagged her mother and constantly tried to put her in a temper.

Nevertheless, she was vivacious, excitable, and lovable, and very affectionate to every one. She showed her appreciation of the problem of her management by exclaiming one day, with her arms full of dolls, 'All this family do make me ache'. She was richly imaginative. During an interview with me she drew rapidly and in a scatty way all over the page—figures, nudes, parts of people, odd objects; and in one case she cut a hole out of the belly of a woman. There had been a bout of drawings of nude girls at school.

At school she was said to have instability of character—a weak character and a dominant personality, with a power over others which (they complained) she used to force other children to do wrong, even against their will. She stole and hid food or books. The few existing rules and disciplines were not felt by Margaret to apply to herself. She was a masterhand at prevarication. Yet she would try to intervene on other children's behalf if they were in trouble.

I advised a term at home in spite of the bombing, and during this time Margaret learned to play the violin. She became very difficult over food, and developed a fear of being shut in anywhere. She was now able to go to school in the country, but the first term was very difficult. She was always on the point of running away, and for this she planned to steal—she always needed thirty shillings. At this point Margaret developed a dependence on a psychiatric social worker who happened to be available locally, whom she called frequently on the telephone, and by whom she was visited every evening at a given time for some weeks. A considerable degree of dependence developed. Here was a critical period, but in this way the girl was enabled to gain confidence to stay at school, and her mother came to visit her at half-term. Gradually she developed her many positive qualities. At 13 the sequel to her earlier phobia of buses was a wish to be a bus conductress. She played her violin at a concert and was said to have a great appreciation of beauty. She played tennis with ability. Moreover the paranoid quality in her personality seemed to be 'swept away' at the time when she had pneumonia at school, and her mother, who had always had to promise to turn up if Margaret was ill, now felt that she could leave the child to be looked after at school. Margaret was able to accept being well looked after and brought round to health. Her last year at school was a happy one, and she made many friends. With her parents' strong directing help at home she was able to gain the School Certificate.

After leaving school Margaret went to be trained to work with children. The early stages of her career were precarious; she was the sort of person that gets stolen from, and she managed to get any ill-treatment and neglect that could be discovered. The parents took up every point and dealt with it on a realistic basis, and naturally some complaints were found to have justification. Margaret was on the point of giving up all the time, and in various ways the parents had to be constantly engaged in dealing with situations and tolerating anxiety. At the age of 19 she seemed to her mother to be at the 17-year-old level. She repeated during her training the sort of troubles that she had produced at school. For instance, she had to be home for a while having treatment for a severe state of round-shoulders, and at home she was exceedingly difficult to handle. She was slack, wasted her time, and was discontented. This went on for nearly six months, with constant illnesses. She became ill whenever her parents went away on holiday, but she did not let them know until their return.

At her training school she was good with children, but jealous and a tax on the staff. She developed a technique whereby the parents frequently found themselves spending a little more on her in order to lessen an awkward tension. She always needed the best, regardless of the parents' means, and would wear only clothes that were perfect. She even realised that she 'made hell' at home. Nevertheless, with a push, she was always just able to succeed at times of test. Actual stealing and being stolen from ceased, and lying was replaced by a compulsion to get pity. The best thing in her life was her music. She repeatedly told her mother that she was mean, and she would boast of how her smart friends spoiled her. As before, so here, the turning-point came when she had an illness and was nursed at the training school instead of at home. This illness was probably of neurotic origin.

By now the mother was 72 and feeling the strain.

After recovery from the illness, Margaret became more intensely interested in her work with children, and was at last regarded as a promising student, although some of her former difficulties remained. Eventually she said to her mother, 'It may be a consolation to you to know that now I would not leave the school for anything'. At long last the mother felt rewarded for everything she had been through, since the word consolation showed that Margaret knew what a trouble she had had to be. At this time Margaret started reading serious literature. In the end, after nearly giving up time after time, and needing constant encouragement, she passed her examinations first class and took two additional examinations, on the ground that her brother Peter said she ought to. Immediately she took a job, having carefully sorted applications and selected just the right one, and she is now looking after a child in a household in which there is enough money for some extras. She is herself an attractive young woman of 22, with a flair for dressing well, and she is a responsible and well-trained person. Here in her first job, looking after a 'perfect' baby, she seems to have found something corresponding to what is, I suppose, her idealised conception of her real parents. Her adoptive parents with the means at their disposal could not compete, which may have been fortunate.

A recent story illustrates her attitude. One day Margaret found herself unable to tolerate the rude and disagreeable behaviour of a maid towards the mother, and reprimanded her. The maid retorted, 'But you're often rude to her yourself.' Margaret said, 'That's different; *she's my mother.*'

THEORETICAL SUMMARY

The first child, Peter, adopted at ten months, is now 26 years. He had had an ordinary good infancy experience. He had been breast-fed by his own mother and weaned by her, and during most of this period the mother had no intention of parting with the child. He had had to deal with the disturbance due to change of environment and loss of real mother at ten months, but by this date he had already been weaned and had become established as an individual in his own right. In Peter's case, therefore, the problems were more those that belong to ordinary child care than to adoption in particular. In my personal opinion it is best either that a child is brought through the early stages of infant care by the real mother, as in this case, or else that the adoptive parents should take the child over as early as possible in infancy, perhaps during the first few days. But it is probably rare for a child to have so good a pre-history on adoption at ten months as Peter had.

The second child, Margaret, adopted at eleven months, and now aged 22 years, was already a disturbed child at adoption. In other words, her early infancy management was relatively muddled (although not as muddled as might have been the case). Margaret therefore started adoption with a handicap :

(a) The relative environmental failure in a general way deprived the child of that early good start in personal development which good enough environmental provision makes possible.

(b) There was nevertheless some *organisation* of an illness pattern at eleven months, indicating a certain strength of Ego. The illness pattern was on a paranoid basis, that is to say there was an artificial rearrangement of objects in the sense that those that felt bad were placed outside in the world, and those that felt good were collected together within. The adoptive parents therefore had to deal with an ill child. By steady and simplified environmental provision the parents gradually corrected the early failure, at any rate to a considerable extent. The child's illness pattern made it possible for her to express her suspicion of love in terms of substitutes, namely money, treatments for illnesses, a claim on the mother for tolerance, or an expectation of ill-treatment. The child's capacity for love, and for being loved, appeared in various positive qualities, and in her music and her flair for dressing well. The child is now 22, and engaged in a job which involves identification with a mother caring for an infant. There are certainly troubles in store, and there is a long road between the present state of affairs and the child's ability to take on the responsibility for a family of her own. But the parents are still able to take part in this girl's development, and there is in addition the adoptive brother, who has a deep sense of responsibility for her, and who is there as an insurance in the background as the parents grow older.

The achievement in this case of the adoption of two children is the more remarkable in that the mother was 48 when she adopted Peter, and 53 when she adopted Margaret, and the father was only a few years younger.

This case description is given as a token of my respect for them in their achievement.

PART II

Children Under Stress

INCLUDING WARTIME BROADCASTS

1

Children in the War
[1940]

To understand the effect of war on children it is first necessary to know what capacity children have for the understanding of war and of the causes of war, and of the reasons by which we justify our fighting. Of course, what is true of one age group is not true of another. This may be rather obvious, but it is important, and I will try to put into words what it implies.

What is also important is the variation between one child and another, apart from age differences. This I will also try to describe.

Age Group Variations

Tiny children are only indirectly affected by war. They are scarcely wakened from sleep by guns. The worst effects come from separation from familiar sights and smells, and perhaps from mother, and from loss of contact with father, things which often cannot be avoided. They may however come into contact with mother's body more than they would ordinarily do, and sometimes they have to know what mother feels like when she is scared.

Quite soon, however, children begin to think and talk in terms of war. Instead of talking in terms of fairy stories that have been read and repeated, the child uses the currency of the adults around him, and his mind is full of aeroplanes, bombs, and craters.

The older child leaves the age of violent feelings and ideas, and enters a period of waiting for life itself, a period which is the teacher's heyday, since ordinarily a child between 5 and 11 years is longing to be taught and told what is accepted as right and good. In this period, as is well known, the *real* violence of war can be very distasteful, while at the same time aggression appears regularly in play and fantasy with romantic colouring. Many never leave this stage of emotional development, and the result may be harmless, and may even lead to highly successful accomplishment. Actual war, however, seriously upsets the lives of adults who have stuck here, and this gives the cue to those who have charge of children who are in this 'latency' period of emotional development to select and enlarge upon the non-violent side of war. One teacher has described how this may be done through the use of war news in the geography lesson : this town in Canada is interesting because of evacuation, this country is important because it contains oil or has a good harbour, that country may become important next week because it grows wheat or supplies manganese. The violent side of war is not stressed.

A child in this age group does not understand the idea of a fight for freedom, and indeed could be expected to see a great deal of virtue in what a Fascist or Nazi regime is *supposed* to provide, in which someone who is idealised controls and directs. This is what is happening inside the child's own nature at this age, and such a child would be liable to feel that freedom meant licence.

In the majority of schools the stress would be laid on the Empire, the parts coloured red in the maps of the world, and it is not easy to show why children in the latency period of emotional development should not be allowed to idealise (since idealise they must) their own country and kind.

A child of 8 or 9 years might be expected to play at 'English and Germans' as a variation on the theme of 'Cowboys and Indians', or 'Oxford and Cambridge'. Some children show a preference for one or other side, but this may vary from day to day, and many do not much care. Then comes an age at which it is expected that, if the game is one of 'English and Germans', the child shall prefer to identify with his own country. The wise teacher is not in a hurry to find this.

Discussion of the case of the child of twelve and over becomes complex because of the great effects which result from the delay of puberty. As I have said, many people partially retain the qualities that belong to the so-called latency period, or return to these qualities after a furtive attempt to attain a more mature development. For them one can say that the same principles hold as for the real latency child, except that it is with more and more misgiving that we tolerate them. For instance, whereas it is quite normal for a nine-year-old to like to be controlled and directed by an idealised authority, it is less healthy if the child is 14. One can often see a definite and conscious hankering after the Nazi or Fascist regime in a child who hovers on the brink, fearing to launch away into puberty, and such a hankering should obviously be treated with sympathy, or be sympathetically ignored, even by those whose more mature judgment on political matters makes admiration of a dictator an ugly thing. In a certain number of cases this pattern sets in as a permanent alternative to puberty.

After all, the Authoritarian regime has not sprung out of nothing; in one sense it is a well-recognised way of life found in the wrong age group. When it claims to be mature it has to stand the full test of reality, and this brings out the fact that the idealisation in the Authoritarian idea is itself an indication of something unideal, something to be feared as a controlling and directing power. The onlooker can see this bad direction at work, but the young devotee himself presumably only knows that he blindly follows where his idealised leader leads.

Children who are really coming to grips with puberty and the new ideas which belong to that period, who are finding a new capacity for the enjoyment of personal responsibility, and who are beginning to cope with an increased potential for destruction and construction, may find some help in war and war news. The point is that grown-ups are more honest in wartime than in peacetime. Even those who cannot acknowledge personal responsibility for this war mostly do show that they can hate and fight. Even *The Times* is full of stories that can be enjoyed like an exciting adventure story. The B.B.C. likes to link Hun-hunting with the pilot's breakfast, dinner, and tea, and exploits over Berlin are called picnics, though each exploit brings about death and destruction. In wartime we are all as bad and as good as the adolescent in his dreams, and this reassures him. We as an adult group may recover sanity, after a spell of war, and the adolescent, as an individual, may one day become able easily to pursue the arts of peace, though by then he will be no longer a youth.

The adolescent, therefore, may be expected to enjoy actual war bulletins as given to adults, which he can take or leave as he pleases. He may hate them, but by then he knows what it is we are so eager about, and this clears his conscience when he discovers that he has himself the capacity to enjoy wars and cruelty as they turn up in his fantasy. Something corresponding to this could be said of adolescent girls, and the differences between boys and girls in this respect very much need working out.

Variations according to Diagnosis

It seems strange to use the word diagnosis in the description of presumably normal children, but it is a convenient word for emphasising the fact that children differ from each other widely, and that differences according to the diagnosis of character types can cut right across differences that belong to classification by age groups.

I have already indicated this by pointing out the great allowance that has to be made at such an age as 14, according to whether or not the child has plunged into puberty dangers, or has shrunk back from them to the more sure, if less interesting, position of the latency period. Here we are reaching the borderline of psychological illness.

Without attempting to distinguish between well and ill, one can say that children can often be grouped according to the particular tendency or difficulty they can be seen to be contending with. An obvious case would be the child with an anti-social tendency for whom war news tends to come, whatever his or her age, as an expected thing, something he misses if it is not there. In fact, such children's ideas are so terrible that they dare not think, and they deal with them by acting out things that are less bad than those they might dream about. The alternative is for them to hear about other people's awful adventures. For them the thriller is a sleeping-draught, and the same may be said of war news if it is sufficiently lurid.

In another group is the timid child, who easily develops a strong passive-masochistic trend, or who suffers from a capacity to feel persecuted. I think that such a child is worried by war news and by the idea of war, largely because of his fixed idea that the good loses. He feels defeatist. In his dreams the enemy shoots down the fellow-countryman, or at any rate the tussle is never ending, with no victory, and developing more and more cruelty and destruction.

In another group is the child on whose shoulders the burden of the world seems to lie, the child who is liable to feel depressed.

Out of this group come those capable of the most valuable constructive effort, whether it take the form of the care of the younger children, or of the production of what is valuable in one or other art form. For such children the idea of war is awful, but they have already experienced it within themselves. No despair is new to them, nor any hope. They worry about war just as they worry about their parents' separation or the illness of their grandmother. They feel they ought to be able to put it all right. For such children I suppose that war news is terrible when really bad, and exhilarating when really reassuring. Only there will be times when despair or exhilaration over their internal affairs will show as moods, irrespective of the situation in the real world. I think these children suffer more from the variability of the grown-ups' moods than from the vagaries of the war itself.

It would be too big a task to enumerate all the character types here, and unnecessary, since what I have written suffices to show how the diagnosis of the child affects the problem of the presentation of war news in schools.

Background for News

It may have become clear from what has been said under these first two headings that in considering this problem we must know as much as possible of the ideas and feelings that the child already and naturally owns, on top of which the war news will be planted. This unfortunately complicates matters considerably, but nothing can alter the fact that the complexity does in fact exist.

Every one knows that the child is concerned with a personal world, which is only to a limited extent conscious, and which requires a deal of managing. The child deals with personal wars within his or her own breast, and if his outward demeanour is in conformity with civilised standards this is only the result of a big and constant struggle. Those who forget this are repeatedly bewildered by evidences of breakdown of this civilised superstructure, and by unexpectedly fierce reactions to quite simple events.

It is sometimes imagined that children would not think of war if it were not put into their heads. But any one who takes the trouble to find out what goes on beneath the surface of a child's mind can discover for himself that the child already knows about greed, hate, and cruelty, as about love and remorse, and the urge to make good, and about sadness.

73

Little children understand the words good and bad very well, and it is of no value to say that to them these ideas are only in fantasy, since their imaginary world can seem more real to them than the external world. I must make it clear at this point that I am talking of largely unconscious fantasy, and not of fantasying or day-dreaming, or consciously operated story-making.

It is only possible to come to understand children's reactions to the giving of war news by first studying, or at any rate allowing for, the immensely rich inner world of each child, which forms the background for whatever is painted in from to-day's external reality bulletin. As the child matures he becomes more and more able to sort out external or shared reality from his own personal inner reality, and to let each enrich the other.

Only when the teacher really knows the child personally is the stage properly set for making the best use of war and war news in education. Since, in practice, the teacher can know the child only to a limited extent, it would be a good plan to allow the children to do other things—read or play dominoes—or to wander off altogether whilst the B.B.C. war news is being given.

It seems to me, therefore, that these reports usefully start us off in a study of an immense problem, and perhaps our first task is just to realise and recognise its immensity. The subject is certainly worth study, for, like many another, it carries us far beyond everyday educational procedure, and reaches down to the origins of war itself, and to the fundamentals of the emotional development of the human being.

2

The Deprived Mother [1]
[1940]

PARENTS are specially attuned to child care, and, to understand the problems of the mothers of children who have been evacuated, it is necessary first of all to recognise that feelings in general about children are not the same as the special feelings of parents towards their own children.

What makes life worth while for many men and women is the experience of the first decade of married life, when a family is being built up, and while the children are still in need of those contributions to personality and character which the parents can give. This is true generally, but it is particularly true of those who manage their household themselves, without servants, and of those whose economic position, or educational standard, sets a limit to the quantity and quality of the interests and distractions available for them. For such parents, to give up the daily and hourly contact with their children is likely to be a serious trial.

One mother said, 'We would give up our children for three months, but if it is to be for longer, perhaps even for three years, what is the point of life?' And another said, 'All I have to care for now is the cat, and my one distraction is the pub.' These are calls for help which should not go unanswered.

Most tales about parents whose children have been evacuated show no appreciation of this simple truth. For instance, the opinion has been expressed that mothers are having such a good time, being free to flirt, to get up late, to go to the cinema, or to go to work and earn good money, that they will certainly not want to have their children with them again. No doubt there are cases on which this is fair comment, but such an idea does not apply to

[1] Written at the time of the first evacuation.

the majority of mothers; and when such comment is true on the surface it is by no means necessarily true in a deeper sense, for it is a well-known human characteristic to become flippant under threat of a grief that cannot be tolerated.

No one would suggest that the bearing and the bringing up of children is all honey, but most people do not expect life to be sweet without bitter; they ask that the bitter part shall be to some extent of their own choosing.

The city-dwelling mother is asked, advised, and indeed pressed to give up her children. Often she feels bullied into compliance, not being able to see that the harshness of the demand comes from the reality of the danger from bombs. A mother can be surprisingly sensitive to criticism; so powerful is the latent sense of guilt about the possession of children (or of anything valuable, for that matter) that the idea of evacuation first tends to make a mother unsure of herself and willing to do whatever she is told, regardless of her own feelings. One can almost hear her saying, 'Yes, of course, take them away, I was never worthy of them; air raids are not the only danger, it is my own self that fails to provide them with the home they ought to have.' It will be understood that she does not consciously feel all this, she only feels confused or stunned.

For this and for other reasons the initial compliance with the scheme must not be expected to last. Eventually the mothers recover from the first shock, and then a great deal has to happen before the compliance can be said to have changed into co-operation. As time goes on the fantasy changes, and the real gradually becomes clearly defined.

If one makes the attempt to put oneself in the mother's place one immediately asks the question : why, in fact, are children being taken from the risk of air raids at such great expense and trouble? Why are parents being asked to make such big sacrifices?

There are alternative answers.

Either the parents themselves really want their children to be taken out of danger, whatever their own feelings, so that the authorities are merely acting on the parents' behalf; or else the State puts more value on the future than on the present, and has decided to take over the care and management of the children, apart altogether from the feelings and wishes and needs of the parents.

As is natural in a democracy, the feeling has been to regard the first alternative as valid.

For this reason evacuation has been voluntary, and has been allowed to some extent to fail. In fact there has been some attempt, even if a half-hearted one, to understand the mother's side of the question.

It is worth remembering that children are cared for and educated not only to give them a good time, but also to help them to grow up. Some of them will in turn become parents. It is reasonable to hold the view that parents are as important as children, and that it is sentimental to assume that parents' feelings should necessarily be sacrificed for children's welfare and happiness. Nothing can compensate the average parent for loss of contact with a child, and of responsibility for the child's bodily and intellectual development.

It is claimed that it is the vastness of the problem, and of the organisation required to deal with mass evacuation, that limits the share that the parents can be allowed in such things as the choosing of billets. Most parents are able to see this. It is, however, the purpose of this article to point out that however much the authorities may attempt to make rules and regulations intended to be of general application, evacuation remains a matter of a million individual human problems, each different from the others, and each urgently important to someone. As an example, a mother may herself be a student of evacuation problems, and in touch with all its many difficulties, yet she will not be helped by such knowledge to tolerate loss of contact with her own child.

Children change rapidly. At the end of the years that this war may last many children will no longer be children, and all toddlers of the present day will have grown out of the stage of quick emotional development into that of intellectual development and emotional marking-time. It makes no sense to talk of postponing getting to know a child, especially a little child.

Furthermore, mothers appreciate one thing that those who are not so close to the child are apt to forget, that time itself is very different according to the age at which it is experienced. A holiday which the grown-ups hardly noticed may have seemed like a huge chunk of life to the children, and it is almost impossible to convey to an adult the length of time that three years may seem to the evacuated child. It really is a big proportion of what the child knows of life, equivalent perhaps to twenty-five years in the life of an adult of 40 or 50. Recognition of this makes a mother still more anxious to lose nothing of her chance of motherhood.

Investigation, therefore, of any one detail of the whole problem of evacuation uncovers individual problems that are important, even urgent, in their own way.

Working now on the basis that the parents' ultimate wishes are represented by the authorities who are thus acting for the parents, it is possible to see what are the complications that are likely to ensue.

It is commonly believed, even by parents themselves, that all would be well if only their children were to be well looked after; that the children, if they were sufficiently developed emotionally to stand the separation, might actually benefit from the change; surely the children would experience a new kind of home, widen their interests, and perhaps get a contact with country life which is denied to town and even to suburban children.

There is no good in denying, however, that the situation is a complex one and that parents cannot by any means be relied on to *feel* assured of their children's well-being.

This is an old and familiar story, but one that seldom fails to upset and astonish those who have children in their care away from their homes. Parents readily complain about the treatment of their children while away, and easily believe any story a child may invent about ill-treatment and especially about bad feeding. The fact that a child arrives home from a convalescent home in the pink of condition does not prevent a mother from lodging a complaint that her child has been neglected. These complaints, on being followed up, very seldom lead to the discovery of really bad convalescent homes; similar complaints in the case of evacuated children's billets may be expected, and are natural enough if the mother's doubts and fears are taken into account. A mother is expected to dislike any one who neglects her child, but she might quite as reasonably be expected to dislike any one who looks after her child better than she does herself; for such good care rouses her envy or jealousy. It is her own child and, quite simply, she wants to be her own child's mother.

It is not difficult to imagine what happens. A child comes home on holiday and quickly senses an atmosphere of tension when asked some detail. 'Did Mrs. So-and-so give you a glass of milk before bed?' The child may be relieved to be able to answer 'No' and so to please mother without dissembling. The child is in a conflict of loyalties and is puzzled. Which is better, home or away? In some cases the defence against this very conflict has been prepared by a refusal of food at the billet during the first and last days there. If the mother shows quite a lot of relief the child is tempted to add a few details imaginatively. The mother now begins really to feel that there has been neglect, and pumps the child for more information. Tension is now high and rising, and the child scarcely dares look back to see what has been said. It is safer to stick to a few details, and to repeat them whenever the subject is brought up. And so the mother's suspicion is built up until in the end she lodges a complaint.

The difficult situation arises from two sources; the child feels it would be disloyal to report happiness and good feeding, and the mother nurses a hope that the foster-mother compares unfavourably with herself. There are moments when a vicious circle of suspicion on the part of the actual parent, and resentment on the part of the foster-mother, may easily be set up. That moment passed, the way is open for friendship and understanding between these potential rivals.

This may all seem very unreasonable to the outsider, who can afford to be reasonable, but logic (or reasoning that denies the existence or importance of *unconscious* feelings and conflicts) is not enough when a mother has her child taken from her. Even though a deprived mother really wishes to co-operate with the scheme, these unconscious feelings and conflicts must be given their due weight.

In the periods intervening between the moments of suspicion, mothers just as easily tend to over-estimate the reliability and goodness of the billets, and to believe that their children are safe and well cared for without knowledge of the real facts. Human nature works that way.

Nothing is so likely to arouse jealousy in the mother as the provision of exceptional care. She may be able to hide her jealousy even from herself, but if she has cause for worry lest her child be neglected, she has no less cause for worry lest her child shall get accustomed while away to standards which cannot be maintained after his or her return. This is especially likely to be true when this standard is only a grade higher than that in the home, for if the billet is a castle the whole experience is lifted into the realm of a dream.

The way in which little points can become magnified is illustrated by the following incident.

A mother complained about a foster-mother, and it turned out that the complaint was little more than this, that the foster-mother was generous and owned a sweet shop, whereas the mother herself not only could not afford to give the child a lot of sweets, but also withheld them because she felt they were bad for the child's teeth.

These problems are not different from those of everyday life. When a relation or a friend is indulgent to a child the mother suffers by being forced into the role of strict and even cruel parent, and the home situation is frequently eased when a child meets firmness elsewhere.

It will be appreciated that it is not wise to advertise to a mother the wonderful food the child is getting, and all the other special advantages that the billet may have over the child's home. Nor is it wise to say (especially when it is true) that the child is happier in the billet than at home. There can be, in fact, quite a lot of triumph hidden behind such reports.

Yet parents expect and should surely receive reports, written without triumph, and with the object of enabling them to continue sharing responsibility for their children's welfare. If contact is not maintained, imagination is apt to fill in details *on a fantastic basis*.

In a further study of the deprived mother, it is necessary to go beyond what she can be expected to know about herself. An important thing to be reckoned with is that a mother not only wants children, she also *needs* them. In setting out to bring up a family she organises her anxieties, as well as her interests, so as to be able to mobilise as much as possible of her emotional drive to that one end. She finds value in being continuously bothered by her children's crying needs, and this holds good even if she openly complains of her family ties as a nuisance.

She may never have given thought to this aspect of her motherhood experience until, when the children have gone, she first finds herself the possessor of a quiet kitchen, the captain of a vessel with no crew. Even if her personality has sufficient flexibility to allow her to adjust to such a new situation, this change-over of interests requires time.

She can perhaps take a brief holiday from her children without any rearrangement of her vital interests; but there is a period of

time beyond which she can no longer do without someone or something that she feels to be worth while caring for, and wearing herself
out for; she also begins to seek some alternative way of exercising
power usefully.

In the ordinary way a mother gradually accustoms herself to new
interests as the children grow up, but mothers are asked in the
present time of war to accomplish this difficult process in a few
weeks. It is not to be wondered at that they often fail, either
becoming depressed, or else illogically insisting on the children's
return.

There is another side of this same problem. Mothers may have
a similar difficulty in taking their children back after they have
reorganised their interests and anxieties to deal with the experience
of peace and quiet in the home. Again, the time factor must be
allowed for. This second reorganisation may easily be more difficult
than the first, for there will be a period, however brief, on the children's return, in which the mother will have to pretend to her
children that she is ready for them, and pretend that she needs them
as she did before they went away; she will have to pretend because,
at first, she will not feel ready for them. Time is required for her
to adjust her inner thoughts, as well as the outer arrangement of
the home, to their reception.

For one thing, the children really have changed, they are older
and they have had new experiences; and also she has had all sorts
of thoughts about them while they have been away, and she needs
to live with them a little while before she can get to know them
again as they really are.

This fear of having to make a big and painful adjustment, with
risk of failing in the attempt, drives mothers to go and snatch their
children from their billets, regardless of the feelings of those who,
as likely as not, have done everything in their power for the children's good. It is as if the mothers are in a play in which they
have been robbed, and in which their clear duty is to rescue the
children from ogres; as rescuers they reassure themselves of the
existence and strength of their own parental love.

Special attitudes of more abnormal mothers ought also to be
described. There is the mother who feels her child is only good
when personally controlled by herself. Being unable to recognise
the child's innate positive qualities she warns the prospective foster-

parents to expect trouble, and cannot understand when the child is found to behave normally. Then also there is the mother who runs down her child, just as an artist depreciates his picture and is therefore the worst person in the world to sell it. She, like the artist, fears both praise and blame, and she forestalls criticism by her own undervaluation of her belongings.

SUMMARY

Within the limits of this article I have tried to show that when a child is taken from parents the very strongest feelings are aroused.

Those who are concerned with the problems of the evacuation of children must see the mothers' problems as well as those of the foster-mothers if they are to understand what they are doing.

To look after children may be hard and exacting work, it can feel like a war job. But just to be deprived of one's children is a poor kind of war work, one which appeals to hardly any mother or father, and one that can only be tolerated if its unhappy side is duly appreciated. For this reason it is necessary really to make the effort to find out what it feels like to be a mother stranded without her child.

3

The Evacuated Child

[1945]

I T seems a long time since the first evacuation, and it can be assumed that the acute problems belonging to evacuation have mostly solved themselves by now. But I want to remind you of some of your experiences, talking especially to foster-parents.

A great spread of much-needed understanding of child care could follow as a consequence of all that people have been through. Almost every household in Great Britain was affected by evacuation, and indeed every woman has her own evacuation story that sums up her experience and her view of the whole matter. It seems to me that it would be a pity if all this experience were to be wasted. I shall talk chiefly to those who succeeded in keeping their evacuee over a period of years, because I think it is you who stand to gain most by any attempt to put into words what you have been doing.

I suppose that when there was success you will agree that you were fortunate in the child sent to you. The boy or girl had a certain degree of belief in people. You had material to work on; it really is impossible to succeed in this work if the child cannot contribute because of being too ill, too mentally unstable, or too insecure to find goodness in what you have to offer.

A child was billeted on you who had already started satisfactorily in his emotional development. This was going on well before you received the child into your home, and, if you have kept him over a long period, it means that you have enabled the growth of his personality to continue, just as you have enabled his body to go on growing by providing food.

The bodily care of a child is a big thing in itself. To keep a child in health and free from bodily illness is something which needs constant watching, and in the course of a long evacuation period there must have been times when you had to take responsibility for bodily illness, something which is much more difficult to do when the child is not your own than when the child is yours. You cared for the child's body; but the evacuation brought home to many who had not realised it before that this is only part of that larger thing; the care of the whole child, the whole child who is a human being with a constant need for love and imaginative understanding. The point is that you have done so much more than provide food, clothes, and warmth.

But even this was not enough. The child came from home, and you have taken the child into your home. And home seems to get behind the idea of love. It might be possible for someone to love a child and yet to fail because a child got no feeling that he was at home. I think that the point is that if you make a *home* for a child you provide a little bit of the world that the child can understand and can believe in, in moments when love fails. For love must fail at times, at least superficially. There must be times, every now and again, when a child irritates and annoys and earns an angry word, and it is at least equally true that grown-up people, even the best, have moods and times of irritability, when for an hour or so they cannot be relied on to deal with a situation with fairness. If there is a feeling of homeliness, the relationship between a child and the grown-ups can survive periods of misunderstanding. So I think we can assume that if you have kept your evacuee for a long time you have taken the child into your home, which is such a different thing from letting him into your house, and the child has responded and has used your home as a home. The child in your home came to believe in you, and gradually became able to transfer some feelings from his mother to you, so that in a sense you did become temporarily the child's mother. If you have succeeded you must have found some way of dealing with the very tricky relationship between you and the real parent, and something like the George Medal ought to be struck for the parents and foster-parents who have managed to come to terms, and even to form friendships, when there has been so much cause for mutual misunderstanding.

And now what about the child who has suddenly been uprooted, seemingly turned out of his own home and dumped down among strangers? No wonder he needed special understanding.

At first, when the children were sent away from the danger zones, there was usually with them the teacher who already knew them well. This teacher formed a link with the home town, and in most cases a bond developed between the children and the teacher much stronger than that of the ordinary teacher-pupil relationship. It is indeed scarcely possible to think of the first evacuation scheme without these teachers, but the full story of those exciting, and in some ways tragic, first hours and days of evacuation has yet to be written.

Sooner or later every child had to look the fact fully and squarely in the face, to realise that he was away from home, and lonely. What happened at that point depended on the age of the child, as well as on the kind of child he was, and the kind of home he came from, but essentially the same problem had to be met by all : either the child had to settle down and accept the new home, or else he had to hang on to the idea of his own home, treating the foster-home as a place where he was to stay for rather too long a holiday.

Many children settled in and seemed to present no problem at all, but perhaps more can be learned from the difficulties than from the easy successes. For instance, I should say that the child who settled in right away, and who never seemed to worry about home at all, was not necessarily in a good way. There could easily be an unnatural acceptance of the new conditions, and in some cases this lack of home-sickness proved in the end to be a snare and a delusion. It is so very natural for a child to feel that his own home is best, and that his own mother's cooking is the only good cooking. More usually you found the child in your care took a long time, perhaps a very long time, to settle in. I am suggesting that this was good. Time had to be taken. He remained frankly anxious about his home and his parents, and indeed he had good cause to be anxious, since the danger to the home was real and well known, and as the stories of bombing began to go the rounds the justification for worry grew. Children from bombed areas did not just go about looking exactly like the local children, and joining in all the playing; they tended to keep apart, and to live on letters and parcels from home, and the occasional visits, visits that often led to so much upset that foster-parents wished them rarer still. It was not so pleasant for foster-parents when the children behaved in this way, and refused food, and moped about most of the time wishing to be home sharing the parents' dangers instead of enjoying the benefits of a stay in the country. All this was not really an unhealthy thing, but to understand it we must look deeper. The real worry about bombs was not all.

A child has only a limited capacity for keeping alive the idea of someone who is loved when there is no opportunity for seeing and talking to that person, and that is where the real trouble lies. For days or even weeks all is well, and then the child finds he cannot feel that his mother is real, or else he keeps on having the idea that father or brothers or sisters are coming to harm in some way. This is the idea in his mind. He has dreams with all sorts of frightening struggles which point to the very intense conflicts in his mind. Worse than that, after a while he may find that he has no strong feelings at all. All his life he has had live love feelings, and he has come to rely on them, taking them for granted, being buoyed up by them. Suddenly, in a strange land, he finds himself without the support of any live feelings at all, and he is terrified by this. He does not know he will recover if he can wait. Perhaps there is some teddy or doll or piece of clothing rescued from the home towards which he continues to have some feelings, and this then becomes tremendously important to him.

This threat of loss of feelings, which comes to children who are too long away from all that they love, often leads to rows. The children start milling around looking for trouble, and when someone gets angry there is genuine relief; but this relief is not lasting. In evacuation, children have just had to endure these distressing periods of doubt and uncertainty, being unable to go home, and it must be remembered that they were not just away at a sort of boarding-school, coming home for holidays. They had to find a new home away from home.

You, as guardians of the children, had to deal with all sorts of symptoms of this distress, including the well-known bed-wetting, aches and pains of one kind and another, skin irritations, unpleasant habits, even head-banging, anything by which the child could regain the feeling of the sense of reality. If one recognises the distress that underlies these symptoms one easily sees how futile it must be to punish a child for them; a better treatment always lies at hand, namely, to help the child by your demonstrative love and imaginative understanding.

It was at such a time, surely, that your evacuee looked to you and your home, which was at any rate real to him. Without you, as we know from all the failures, he either would have gone home to real danger, or else he was liable to become disturbed and distorted in his mental development, with a strong likelihood of getting into trouble. It was just then that you did him a great service.

Up to this point the child had been getting to know you, and had been using your house, eating your food. He now looked to you for love and for the feeling that he was loved. In your new position with the child you were not only the person who worked for him, but you were also there to understand him and to help him to keep alive the memory of his own people. You were also there to receive his attempts to give you back something for what you were doing, and you were needed to protect the child in his frightening relationship to the rather strange world around and at school, where the other children were not always friendly. Sooner or later, I suppose, he gained the necessary confidence in the house and the home, and the way you ran it, to enable him to take it for granted, and then, at last, became like one of the family, a village child with the village children, even talking in the local dialect. Many even came to gain through their experiences, but this came as a climax to a complex series of events, and there were many points at which there might have been failure.

And so here you are with a child in your care who has made use of the best you have had to offer, and you ought to know that it is well recognised that what you have done has not been simple or easy, but has been a matter of careful building. Has all this no value beyond the actual good done to one child? One certain value to be got out of evacuation (itself a tragic thing) is that all of you who have succeeded in keeping an evacuee have come to understand the difficulties, as well as the rewards, that belong to caring for other people's children, and you can help others who are doing the same thing. There have always been destitute children, and there have always been foster-parents who have done the sort of work you have been doing, and doing it well. When it comes to the total care of a child, experience is the one thing that counts, and if each one of you who has succeeded with an evacuee is enabled thereby to become an understanding neighbour of a foster-parent of the post-war period, then I think your work will not have ended with the return of your foster child to his real parents.

4

The Return of the Evacuated Child

[1945]

I HAVE already spoken about the evacuated child, and tried to show that where evacuation has been a success this has not been a matter of chance, but in every case something of an achievement. You will have guessed already that I am not likely to say that the return of the evacuated child is a simple and straightforward matter. Indeed I can't say it because I don't believe it. The home-coming of the child who has had a long period from home is well worth thinking out, because careless management at the critical moment can so easily lead to bitterness.

Let me say first, however, that I do respect the feelings of those who do not much like thinking things out. They act best on intuition, and when they talk about what they are to expect to have to deal with next week they become self-conscious, if they do not actually become scared by all the possible snags that they see. Besides, if talking is a substitute for feeling or action, then it is indeed worse than useless. But undoubtedly some people do like to widen their experience by talking and listening, and it must be for such that I speak.

As usual, the trouble is to know where to start, since there are so many different kinds of children, kinds of billet, and kinds of home. At one extreme are the children who will just come home, and settle down easily, and, at the other extreme, there will be children who have settled so well in their foster-homes that the return home order will come as a real shock. In between come all the problems. I cannot describe everything, so I must try to get to the heart of the matter.

Of course the end of evacuation has come already for a great number of children. Whatever I shall have to say could be said better by those who have lived through the experience. My idea is to pass on some of the results of these experiences to those who have yet to welcome their children home. I think I am right in saying that it is not all plain sailing, this renewing acquaintance with one's own children.

The problem has been simplified if mothers and fathers have been able to get, and keep, on friendly terms with the foster-parents. This can never be easy. It is almost as bad to have one's own children well cared for by someone else as it is to have them neglected. In fact it is maddening if you have been a good mother, and then you see your own child wanting to stay with a woman who is a stranger to you, and actually liking the food she cooks. But, in spite of all this, some parents did manage to make friends with their representatives in their child's affections in the country. And if this has meant that the child has often been reminded of you, and of his brothers and sisters and other relations, your work has been made much easier. I come across children who cannot remember what their mothers are like, and who only remember with difficulty the names of their brothers and sisters. Perhaps for whole stretches of years no one has ever troubled to speak to them of those who are nearest and dearest to them, and the past life of those children, as well as the memories of their home, become tucked away somewhere right inside them.

In some cases a sort of preparation for the return home may have been going on all the time, but in others there has been none. In any case the main difficulties are the same, and depend on the fact that when people are separated from one another they don't just go on for ever living for the reunion, and indeed no one would wish for this. If they had not the capacity to recover from painful separation at least to some extent, people would be paralysed.

I have said that there is a limit to the ability of a child to keep alive the idea of someone he loves without contact with that person. The same can be said of parents too, and of every human being to some extent. Mothers had almost as much difficulty as their children, in this respect. They soon began to feel doubts about their children, to have feelings that they were in danger, or that they were ill or sad or even being ill-treated, quite apart from any justification for thinking these things. It is quite natural for people to need to see and be near those whom they love, or else to worry about them. In the ordinary course of events, with the children at home, when a mother is worried she can just call out, or can wait till the next meal time, and the child she is worried about comes up and gives her a reassuring kiss. Close contact between people has its use, and when it is suddenly broken up people (children or adults) have to suffer fears and doubts, and to go on suffering till recovery occurs. Recovery means that in time the mother ceases to feel responsible for her child, at any rate to a large extent. That is the hateful thing about it : evacuation forced parents to give up their concern for their own children. If they hung on to a child, and tried to keep their responsibility when the child was a hundred or more miles away, they probably lived in hell, and moreover they weakened the sense of responsibility that was developing in the foster-parents, who had the advantage of being on the spot. Imagine the conflict in the minds of the average good parent at this time !

There was nothing for it but for the mother to fill her mind with other interests ; perhaps she went to work in a factory or took on civil defence responsibilities, or developed a private life that enabled her to forget from moment to moment her deep grief. In addition to worrying about her children she was often worried about her husband in the forces, and she had to find out how to manage her instincts with a husband forced to be away for an indefinite period. Compared with all this, what a little thing seems the blast of a bomb !

So the children went, and when they went they left a great hole, but in the course of time the gap closed over, and the hole began to be forgotten. Even from a broken heart most people mend up in time, and reluctantly they find new interests where old interests have failed. As I have said, many women went to work, and some had new babies. I even know some who have difficulty in remembering where their children are. If you do not easily write letters it is quite a job to keep track of half a dozen children who are scattered all over the place, each probably changing from billet to billet.

What I want to say now is that when the children come home they are not necessarily going to fall into and fit nicely into the holes they made when they went away, for the simple reason that the hole has disappeared. Mother and child will have become able to manage without each other, and when they meet they will have to start from scratch to get to know each other. This process must take time, and time must be allowed. It is no use mother rushing up to the child and throwing her arms round his neck without looking to see whether he is going to be able to respond sincerely. They can be brutally sincere, can children, and coldness can hurt. Given time, on the other hand, feelings can develop in their natural way, and suddenly a mother may be rewarded by a genuine hug that was worth waiting for. The home is still the child's home, and I think he will be glad to be there in the course of time, if mother can wait.

In the two or three years of separation both mother and child have altered, more especially the child out of whose life three years is a big chunk. It is tragic to think that so many parents have had to miss that fleeting thing, the childhood of their own children. After three years he is the same person, but he has lost whatever characterises the six-year-old, because he is now 9. And then, of course, even if the home has escaped bomb damage, even if it is exactly as it was when the child left, it seems much smaller to him, because he is so much bigger. Added to this, he may have been billeted where there was much more room than there is in his own home in the city, and there may have been a garden, or a farm even, over which he could run about as long as he didn't frighten the cows during milking. It must be difficult to come back from a farm to a room or two in a block of flats. Yet I do believe most children prefer to be home, and they will fit in gradually given time.

During the period of waiting there may be complaints. It must always seem to a mother that when her child makes complaints he is making a comparison between her and the foster-parents. A child shows by his tone of voice that he is disappointed in something. I think it is well to remember that usually he is not comparing home with the foster-home so much as comparing home as he finds it with that which he had built up in his mind while he was away. In a period of separation a good deal of idealisation goes on, and this is the more true the more complete the disunion. I find that boys and girls who have such bad homes that they have to be given care and protection quite regularly imagine they have an absolutely wonderful home somewhere, if only they could find it. That is the main reason why they tend to run away. They are trying to find home. Do you see that while one of the functions of a real home is to provide something positive in the child's life, another function is to correct the child's picture by showing the limitations of reality?

When the child comes home with his rather fantastic expectations he has to suffer disillusionment at the same time as he rediscovers that he really has a home of his own. Again, all this takes time.

So when children complain after they come home, they are often showing that they had constructed a better home in their imaginations while they were away, a home that denied them nothing, and that had no monetary problems and no lack of floor space, in fact a home that only lacked one thing—reality. Real home also has its advantages though, and children have everything to gain if they gradually come to accept it as it is.

The return of the evacuated child is a big part of the evacuation experience, and nothing would be more disheartening to those who have taken trouble to make evacuation work than carelessness at the end. Surely each child ought to be 'shoe-horned' home, and for this there should be someone responsible who knows the child, the foster-parent, and the real home. Sometimes it will be found that the return home on Monday would be disastrous, whereas on Wednesday all would be well. Perhaps mother is ill, or there is a new baby in the offing, or the builders have not yet quite finished repairing the roof and the windows, and a month or two would make all the difference. In not a few cases a child will come home, but will need skilled supervision for a while, and even so may need to return to a hostel for a time where experienced management is available; especially as the children's fathers are not yet home, and a home without father is no place for a spirited boy, or an adolescent girl.

Lastly, we must not forget that for children with difficult mothers evacuation has been something of a godsend. For these children the return home means a return to strain. In an ideal world there would be some help for these children after their return.

It will be a wonderful thing to know that the children of the big cities are back home again, and I for one will be glad to see the streets and parks full again of children who go home to dinner and tea, and who sleep in their own parents' houses. Education will then start to pick up, and when the men and women come back from the fighting there will be Boy Scouts and Girl Guides, and there will be holiday camps and picnics. But in every case there is the moment of return, and I should like to feel I have made it clear that the renewal of contact takes time, and that the management of each return needs to be personally supervised.

5

Home Again
[1945]

A LITTLE boy I know is 9 years old, and he has spent a great
deal of his young life away from his London home. When
he heard about the return of the evacuees because of the end
of the war, he started thinking things out, getting used to the idea
and making plans. Suddenly he announced, 'When I am home in
London I shall get up early every morning and milk the cows.'

Just now, with the official end of evacuation, and with mothers
returning to the care of their own homes from factories, many
parents are welcoming their children back to the big cities. This is
the moment families have been waiting for over a period of years,
and how good it would be if at the same time all the fathers were
able to come home too.

If I am right, many just now are looking at their children,
wondering what they are thinking and feeling, and wondering, too,
whether they are able to provide all the children want and need.
I should like to think round those problems with you for a few
minutes.

Here are the children home again, filling our ears with sounds
that had long been almost dead. People had forgotten that children
are noisy creatures, but now they are being reminded. Schools are
reopening. Parks are spreading themselves for the reception of their
old customers : mothers and prams, and children of all sizes, shapes,
and colours. Back streets have become cricket pitches, with the children gradually adapting themselves to town traffic. Round the
street corners come bands of Nazis or other kinds of gangsters, complete with guns improvised out of sticks, hunters and hunted alike
oblivious of the passer-by. Chalk marks reappear on pavements, to
let little girls know where to hop, and when the weather is good,

and there is nothing else afoot, boys and girls can be seen standing on their heads or on their outstretched arms, with their feet up against a wall.

The most exciting thing of all, according to my way of thinking, is that at meal-times these children run into their own homes to eat meals prepared by their own mothers. The meal at home means so much, both to the mother who takes the trouble to get the food and to prepare it, and to the children who eat it. And then there is the evening bath, or bedtime story, and the good-night kiss; all these things are private and we do not see them, but we are not ignorant. This is the stuff of which home is made.

Indeed, it is out of the seemingly little things in and around home that the child weaves all that a rich imagination can weave. The wide world is a fine place for grown-ups looking for an escape from boredom, but ordinarily children are not bored, and they can have all the feelings they can stand feeling inside their own house, or within a few minutes from the doorstep. The world is mainly important and satisfactory if it grows for each individual out of the street outside the front door, or the yard at the back.

There are some curious people—optimists, I suppose—who heralded evacuation as something that would bring new life to the poor children of the cities. They could not see evacuation as a great tragedy, so they looked to it as one of the hidden blessings of war. But it could never be a good thing to have to take children from their ordinary decent homes. And by home, you know, I do not mean a lovely house with all the modern conveniences. By home I mean the room or two that has become associated in the child's mind with mother and father, and the other children, and the cat. And there is the shelf or cupboard where the toys are kept.

Yes, a child's imagination can find full scope in the little world of his own home and the street outside, and in fact it is the actual reassurance provided by the home itself that frees the child to play, and in other ways to enjoy his ability to enrich the world out of his own head. There is a serious complication here, when we try to think things out, and I will try to explain what it is. I do say that when a child is home he can have the full range of his feelings there, and this can only be good. At the same time, I am not at all happy about the ideas that come into the child's mind about home when he is away from it for a long time. When he is home, he really knows what home is like, and because of this he is free to pretend it is anything he wants it to be for the purposes of his play. And play is not just pleasure—it is essential to his well-being. When he is away, on the other hand, he has no chance to know from minute to minute what his home is like, and so his ideas lose touch with reality in a way that easily frightens him.

It is one thing for a child at home to fight battles round the wall of the house, and then at one o'clock to go in and have dinner. It is another thing to be evacuated, and out of touch, and to be dreaming of murder in the kitchen. It is one thing to stand on one's head in the street for the pleasure of seeing your house upside down before turning in, and it is quite another to be two hundred miles away, feeling convinced the home is on fire, or falling to pieces.

If you are upset when your child complains that home is not as good as he expected it to be, you can rest assured it is not as bad either. If this is true, you will see how much more free a child is when he is home than when he is away. His home-coming can open up a new era of freedom of thought and imagination, provided he can take time to get to feel that what is real *is* real. This does take time, and you must allow for a slow dawning of confidence.

What happens as a child begins to feel free, free to think what he likes, to play what comes into his head, to find the lost parts of his personality? Surely, he also begins to *act* freely as well, to discover impulses that had lain asleep while he was away, and to show them. He begins to be cheeky, to lose his temper, to waste your food, to try to worry you and to interfere with your other interests. He may very likely try out a little thieving, testing how true it is that you are really his mother, and so in a sense what is yours is his. These can all be signs of a step forward in development—the first stage of a sense of security, although maddening from your point of view. The child has had to be his own strict mother and father while away, and you may be sure that he has had to be over-strict with himself to be on the safe side, unless he has failed to stand the strain, and has got into trouble in his billet. Now, however, at home with you, he will be able to take holidays from self-control, for the simple reason that he will leave the business of control to you. Some children have been living in artificial and over-done self-control for years, and it can be assumed that when they begin to let mother take over control once more they are going to be a bit of a nuisance from time to time. That is why it would be so good if father could be home just now.

I believe that some mothers are genuinely wondering whether they can give as good in Paddington and Portsmouth and Plymouth as the people could give who were looking after their child in the heart of the country, where there were fields and flowers, cows and pigs, fresh vegetables and eggs. Can home compete with the hostel run by experienced wardens, where there were organised games, carpentry for wet days, rabbits increasing their numbers in home made hutches, Saturday expeditions into the surrounding country and visiting doctors caring for the children's bodies and minds? I know that things were often done well both in foster-homes and in hostels, but there are not many who would claim that an ordinary good home can be supplanted. I am sure that, by and large, a child's home, however simple, is more valuable to that boy or girl than any other place to live in.

It is not just the food and shelter that counts, and not even the provision of occupations for spare moments, though, heaven knows, these things are sufficiently important. They may be provided in abundance, and yet the essential must be missing if a child's own parents or adoptive parents or guardians, are not the people taking responsibility for his development. There is the matter which I have mentioned of the need for holidays from self-control. Shall I say that, for a child to be brought up so that he can discover the deepest part of his nature, someone has to be defied, and even at times hated, and who but the child's own parents can be in a position to be hated without there being a danger of a complete break in the relationship?

On the return of the children, those who have managed to keep a home together over these years of bitter separation can now start as father and mother to repair the damage done in their children's development by lack of continuity in their management. You took joint responsibility for their coming into the world, and now I believe you are longing to take up this joint responsibility once more, but this time to enable them to develop into citizens.

As we have seen, this home and family business is not all smiles and kisses ; the return of your boy does not mean that you now have someone who will want to do the shopping for you (except as the impulse takes him), and the return of your daughter does not mean that you have someone who will do your washing-up (except, again, as the impulse takes her). Their return means that your life will be richer, but less your own. There will be few immediate rewards. At times you will wish all of them back again in billets. We all sympathise with you, and at times things may be so difficult that you will need help. You see, some of the children have been so hurt by evacuation that it is beyond the power of parents to manage them. But if you come through, and your children do develop into citizens, you will have done one of the best jobs that can be done. I am told on good authority that it is a wonderful feeling to have one's own children growing up into independence and setting up their own homes, as well as doing work that they enjoy, and enjoying the riches of the civilisation that they must defend and carry along. You will have to be able to be strong in your attitude towards the children, as well as understanding and loving, and if you are going to be strong eventually you may as well start strong. It is rather unfair suddenly to develop strength when it is late, when the child has already begun to test you and try you for reliability.

And now, what about the boy who said he would go home to London and milk the cows? It is easy to see he did not know much about towns and town life, but I do not think that matters much. What I thought when I heard what he said was that he had an idea in mind, quite a good one. He associated going home with something direct and personal. He had watched cows being milked in the farm near his hostel, but he had not been able to go and milk them himself. Now the war is over, home we go, away with the middle-men! Let us milk the cows ourselves! Not a bad motto for returning evacuees. Let us hope that there were a mother and father waiting for Ronald, ready, as he was, for direct affectionate expression, ready with an easy hug to give him the beginning of a new chance to come to terms with a hard world.

6

Residential Management as Treatment for Difficult Children

[1947]

THE EVOLUTION OF A WARTIME HOSTELS SCHEME

I T fell to the lot of the authors to play a part in a wartime scheme
that grew up in a certain county in Britain around the problems presented by children evacuated from London and other
big cities. It is well known that a proportion of evacuated children
failed to settle in their billets; and that whereas some of those went
back home to the air-raids, many of them stayed on and were a
nuisance unless given special conditions of management. As visiting
psychiatrist and resident psychiatric social worker, we formed a
small psychiatric team employed to make a scheme of this kind
work in our county. Our job was to see that the available resources
were actually brought to bear on the problems that arose: one of
us (D.W.W.), as a paediatrician and child psychiatrist whose main
work had been in London, was able to relate such problems as were
specifically related to the war situation to the corresponding problems of peacetime experience.

The scheme that developed was necessarily complex, and it would
be difficult to say that one cog in the wheel was more important
than any other. We are, therefore, describing what happened,
because we have been asked to do so and without claiming to be
specially responsible for its good points; the views expressed are our
own and are given without reference to the other participants in
the scheme.

It could perhaps be said that in our job of seeing that the children
concerned actually did get cared for and treated we also had to

¹ With Clare Britton.

keep the total situation in view; because in every case there was a need for much more to be done than could, in fact, be done; and in each case, therefore, the assessment of the total situation had an important practical bearing. It is this relationship between the work done with each child and the total situation that we especially wish to describe.

It should be mentioned that there was no attempt to make this particular scheme a special case or a pilot model. No grant from a research organisation was sought or accepted. It is not claimed that the scheme with which we happened to be connected was specially good or successful, or that it was better in our county than in other counties. Probably, indeed, the arrangement that grew up in this particular county would have been unsuitable for any other county; and what occurred can be taken as an example of natural adaptation to circumstances.

In fact, a significant feature of such wartime schemes as a whole was the lack of rigid planning, which made it possible for each Ministry of Health Region (indeed, of each county in each region) to adapt to local needs; with the result that at the end of the war there were as many types of scheme as there were counties. This might be thought to be a failure of over-all planning, but in this matter we suggest that opportunity to adapt is of more value than prevision. If a rigid scheme is devised and put into operation, there is an uneconomic forcing of situations where local circumstances do not admit of adaptation; more important still, the people who are attracted to the task of applying a set scheme are very different from those who are attracted by the task of developing a scheme themselves. The attitude of the Ministry of Health, which was responsible for dealing with these matters, seems to us to have called for a creative originality, and therefore for a live interest on the part of all those who had to produce work, and work schemes, according to local needs.[2]

In all work that concerns the care of human beings it is the worker with originality and a live sense of responsibility that is needed. When, as in this task, the human beings are children, children who lack an environment specifically adapted to their individual needs,

[2] It could be said that the Ministry of Health threw a task at a county, watched results, and acted accordingly—a situation which recalls the principle of 'leaderless groups' tasks employed in British Army Officer Selection.

then the worker who loves to follow a rigid plan is unqualified for the task. Any large plan for the care of children deprived of adequate home life must, therefore, be of a type which allows for the fullest degree of local adaptation, and which attracts free-minded people to work it.

THE DEVELOPING PROBLEM

Children evacuated from the big cities were sent to ordinary people's homes. It soon became evident that a proportion of these boys and girls were difficult to billet, quite apart from the complementary fact that some homes were unsuitable as foster-homes.

The billeting breakdowns arising in these ways quickly degenerated into cases of anti-social behaviour. A child who did not do well in a billet either went home and to danger, or else changed billet; several changes of billet indicated a degenerating situation, and tended to be the prelude to some anti-social act. It was at this stage that public opinion became an important factor in the situation : on the one hand there was public alarm, and the activities of courts which represented the usual attitudes towards delinquency, while on the other there was the organising concern of the Ministry of Health, with the developing local interest in providing, for these children, an alternative management designed to prevent their reaching the courts.

The symptoms, in the evacuation breakdown cases, were of all kinds. Bed-wetting and fæcal incontinence had first place, but every possible kind of difficulty was encountered, including stealing in gangs, burning of hay-ricks, train wrecking, truancy from school and from billet, and consorting with soldiers. There were also, of course, the more obvious evidences of anxiety, as well as maniacal outbursts, depressive phases, sulky moods, odd and insane behaviour, and deterioration of personality with lack of interest in clothes and cleanliness.

It was quickly discovered that the symptom-pictures were diagnostically useless, and were merely evidence of distress as a result of ecological failure in the new foster-home. Psychological illness, in the sense of deep endopsychic disturbance apparently unrelated to the current environment, could hardly be recognised as such in the abnormal conditions of evacuation. This situation was complicated by the natural process of mutual choice which led psychologically healthy children to find the good billets.

The initial reaction of the authorities to the emergence of a problem-group of children was to give such children individual psychological treatment, and to provide facilities where they could be placed while receiving treatment. Gradually, however, it became clear that success in providing accommodation of this kind demanded residential management. It emerged, moreover, that such management in itself constituted a therapy. Further, it was important that proper management, as a therapy, should be practical; for it had to be given by relatively unskilled persons—that is, by wardens untrained in psychotherapy, but informed, guided, and supported by the psychiatric team.

As a basic provision, therefore, hostels became organised for residential care of difficult evacuated children. In our county a big disused institution was first used; but from the difficulties of this initial experience the local authority developed the idea of setting up several small hostels, to be run on personal lines,[3] while the appointment of a Psychiatric Social Worker (P.S.W.) who was to be resident in this county arose out of the need to co-ordinate the work of the several hostels, and to build up a body of experience by which the whole scheme could benefit.

In the early stages it was thought that treatment could be given which would enable each child to be re-billeted in a foster-home, but experience showed that this idea was based on an underestimate of the gravity of the trouble. It was, indeed, the psychiatrist's task to direct attention to the fact that these children were seriously affected by evacuation and that nearly all had personal reasons why they could not find good billets to be good; to show, in fact, that these evacuation breakdowns occurred for the most part in children who had originally come from unsettled homes, or in children who had never had in their own homes an example of a good environment.

Therapy by management in residential hostels necessitated a long-stay policy, and the original intentions in regard to hostels had to be modified to allow children to stay for indefinite periods, up to two, three, or four years. In the majority of cases children who were difficult to billet had no satisfactory home of their own, or had experienced the break-up of home, or, just before evacuation, had to bear the burden of a home in danger of breaking up. What they

[3] Cf. the Curtis Report on the Care of Children (1946), H.M.S.O., London.

needed, therefore, was not so much substitutes for their own home as *primary home experiences* of a satisfactory kind.

By a primary home experience is meant experience of an environ ment adapted to the special needs of the infant and the little child without which the foundations of mental health cannot be laid down. Without someone specifically orientated to his needs the infant cannot find a working relation to external reality. Without someone to give satisfactory instinctual gratifications the infant can not find his body, nor can he develop an integrated personality Without one person to love and to hate he cannot come to know that it is the same person that he loves and hates, and so cannot find his sense of guilt, and his desire to repair and restore. Without limited human and physical environment that he can know he cannot find out the extent to which his aggressive ideas actually fail to destroy, and so cannot sort out the difference between fantasy and fact. Without a father and mother who are together, and who take joint responsibility for him, he cannot find and express his urge to separate them, nor experience relief at failing to do so. The emotional development of the first years is complex and cannot be skipped over, and every infant absolutely needs a certain degree of favourable environment if he is to negotiate the essential first stages of this development.

To be of value these primary home experiences belatedly provided in the hostels had to be stable over a period measured in years and not in months; and it can be well understood that the results could never be as good as the ordinary results of good primary home would have been. Success in hostel work, therefore, is to be thought of in terms of lessening the failure of the child's own home.

A corollary of this is that good hostel work must make use of every ounce of value that may still remain in the child's own home.

THE TASK

There are various ways of describing the actual problem:

(1) The protection of the public from the 'nuisance' of children who were difficult to billet.
(2) The resolution of conflicting public feelings of irritation and of concern.
(3) The attempt to prevent delinquency.

(4) The attempt to treat and cure these 'nuisance' children, on the basis of their being ill.

(5) The attempt to help the children on the basis of their hidden suffering.

(6) The attempt to discover the best form of management and treatment for this type of psychiatric case, apart from the specific war emergency.

It will be seen that these various ways of stating the task have to be considered when the question is asked : 'What were the results?' In reply, we might say, in respect to these different formulations of the task :

(1) As far as diminishing the 'nuisance' of difficult children was concerned, 285 children were housed and managed in hostels ; and this was a success except in the case of about a dozen who ran away.

(2) With regard to public irritation, many people felt frustrated at times by the fact that 'offences' of the children were treated as distress signals, instead of indications for punishment ; for example, a farmer whose rick had been burnt down would complain that the culprits seemed to have gained rather than lost by their anti-social act. As to public concern, a great many people who were genuinely concerned by the state of affairs that had developed were relieved by the knowledge that the problem was being tackled. The work of the hostels developed news-value.

(3) Delinquency, in a proportion of cases, was definitely prevented ; as when a child obviously bound for the Juvenile Court before admission into the scheme was seen through to adolescence and a job, without major incident and without Home Office control. In other words, the difficulty was dealt with as a matter of individual and social health, and not merely as a matter of (unconscious) public revenge : the potential delinquency was treated, as it should be, as an illness.

(4) If we regard the problem as one of illness, a small proportion of the children were restored to health, and a fair proportion were brought to a much improved psychological condition.

(5) From the child-patients' point of view, intense suffering was discovered in many of them, as well as hidden or, indeed, open madness ; and in the course of the routine work a great

deal of suffering was shared and to some extent relieved. In a few cases personal psychotherapy could be added, but only enough to show the great need (on the basis of actual suffering) for more personal therapy than can ever be available.

(6) From the sociological angle, the working of the whole scheme gave an indication of the way to deal with potentially anti-social children and insane [4] children, suffering from disorders not produced by war, though evacuation made public the fact of their existence.

THE SCHEME GROWS

Thus the scheme grew out of the acute local needs, and out of the wartime feeling that any cost could be borne, provided the working of the scheme solved the problem in hand. Because of the war, houses could be requisitioned; and in a few months there were five hostels in the group, as well as friendly relations with many others. 'Sick bays' for treatment of physically ill evacuees had, of course, been provided, even in excess of need, and these were available for some of the psychologically ill among the child population of the hostels.

The arrangement was as follows:

The national authority, the Ministry of Health, gave 100 per cent grant to the County Council—that is, accepted full financial responsibility—for this work. The County Council appointed a committee of county residents of standing (with a Deputy Clerk to the Council as Secretary) which was empowered to act as well as to report and recommend to its parent body. A full-time P.S.W. was appointed to work with the visiting psychiatrist, who paid a weekly visit to the county. From then on, the small psychiatric team could undertake to pay that attention to personal matters which is essential in this work; and at the same time, through the regular meetings of the committee, could retain contact with the broad administrative aspect of the situation. In fact, when this stage was reached, the central wide vision of the Ministry became focused on detail.

When this arrangement is examined it will be seen that a circle had been established.

---

[4] The word insane is here used deliberately, for no other word is correct, and the official word 'maladjusted' begs the whole question.

The problem children, because of their nuisance value, had produced a public opinion that would support provision for them which, in fact, catered for their needs.

It would be wrong to say that demand produces supply in human affairs. Children's needs do not produce good treatment, and now the war is over it is very difficult to get such things as hostels for the same children whose needs were met in wartime. The fact is that in peacetime the nuisance value of the distressed children is lessened, and public opinion regains a sleepy indifference. In wartime, evacuation spread the problems of such children over the countryside; it also exaggerated them at a time when the general emotional tension of the community, and the shortage of goods and of manpower, made prevention of damage and theft imperative, and made extra police work unwelcome.

It was not that childhood distress produced child care, but rather that society's fear of the anti-social behaviour from which it suffered at an inopportune moment set in motion a train of events, events that could be used by those who knew of the children's suffering to provide therapy in the shape of long-term residential management, with personal care by an adequate and well-informed staff.

THE PSYCHIATRIC TEAM

Because of the situation described, the task of the psychiatric team turned out to have two aspects: on the one hand, the will of the Ministry had to be implemented; and on the other, the needs of the children had to be met and studied. Fortunately, the direct responsibility of the team was to a committee which liked to be informed about all the details.

In this war experience the voluntary committee remained constant in membership and so developed with the scheme. By being itself stable the committee shared with the psychiatric team a gradual 'growth in the job', so that each success or failure helped to build up a body of experience which had general application and which benefited all the hostels.

To illustrate this, specific instances can be given, even although the main development was in a general way and not capable of illustration.

(1) Gradually, the idea of appointing joint married wardens was adopted. At first this was an experiment, which could only be

made in an atmosphere of mutual understanding, because of the complications arising out of the problems of the wardens' own family and its relation to the hostel children.

(2) The question of corporal punishment was brought up for discussion in the committee, at the appropriate moment, by means of a memorandum; and this led to the formulation of a definite policy.[5]

(3) The idea was put forward, and gradually adopted, that it was better to have one person (in this case the P.S.W.) in the centre of the whole scheme, rather than to have shared responsibility in the administrative office of the scheme, with consequent overlapping and waste of experience because it would not be integrated with total experience.

(4) The psychiatrist was originally appointed to give therapy. This was changed, and he was directed to classify cases before their admission, and to decide on the choice of hostel. Eventually he became the indirect therapist of the children through his regular discussions with the wardens and their staffs.

In these and countless other ways the committee, and the psychiatric team employed by them, retained flexibility and together developed an adaptation to the job.

The importance of this cannot be overestimated and can clearly be seen if we compare this situation with direct relation to a Ministry. In the British Civil Service it is essential that the officials get experience in each of the various departments of government. The consequence is, that if one enters into a personal and understanding relationship with the head of the appropriate department in a Ministry, when the inevitable reshuffles of training and promo-

---

[5] AUTHOR'S NOTE—With regard to corporal punishment, the ruling was that the committee trusted the warden who was appointed, and left to him the right to give corporal punishment. If the committee did not like the way a warden worked the remedy was to get a new warden, and not to interfere directly. A restriction on corporal punishment is quickly found out by the children, and in practice it is a severe handicap to a warden to be curbed by the committee.

In one case, when the committee had doubts, a warden was told to enter each such punishment in a book, which was inspected weekly.

Along with this general policy, there was a drive towards the education of the staff, so that corporal punishment was avoided as much as possible. Through an understanding of the personal difficulties of each child, punishable outbreaks could often be prevented, and in some groups over long periods of time corporal punishment was, in fact, rare.

tion occur, one has to start again with another man. When this has happened several times one finds that whereas one has grown in the job oneself one can no longer feel that the head of the department has grown too; nor can one expect understanding of the details of the work. Since this situation must surely be accepted as an unavoidable phenomenon in large central organisations, one must look to such bodies to give general direction, but to abandon any attempts to keep in touch with detail. And yet in no work is detail more important than in work with children; and so there must always be a 'liaison' committee of interested people who represent the large parent body, and are yet able and willing to stoop to the detail which is the main preoccupation of the actual worker in the field.

It was important that the P.S.W. could take heavy responsibility, and this was made possible by her knowledge that she had the support of the clerk to the Council and the psychiatrist. The latter, by living away from the immediate problems, could discuss the local details without deep emotional involvement, and at the same time, being a medical man, he could accept responsibility for the risks that had to be taken if the best was to be done for the children.

Here is an example of the benefits of technical support and responsibility. A warden rings up the P.S.W. and says, 'A certain boy is on the roof, what shall I do?' He dare not take full responsibility as he is not psychiatrically trained, and he knows the boy has a suicidal tendency. The P.S.W. knows she has the psychiatrist's backing when she says, 'Ignore the boy and take the risk'. The warden knows this is the best treatment, but without backing would have had to give up whatever he was doing, ignore the needs of the other children, perhaps call the local fire brigade, and so do harm to the boy by putting the limelight on him and his escapade. In fact, the result of the advice given to the warden was that at the next meal-time the boy was in his place and no fuss had been made.

The P.S.W. and the visiting psychiatrist provided a psychiatric team that avoided clumsiness by being small, and yet could take responsibility over a wide field. Swift decisions could be made and action be taken within the framework of the powers of the committee by whom they were appointed, and to whom they were directly responsible.

Here are some further examples of detail which proved important:

(1) We found it necessary to take the trouble to gather together the fragments of each child's past history, and to let the child know that one person knew all about him.

(2) No member of the hostel staff could be unimportant. A child might be getting special help from his relationship to the gardener or to the cook. For this reason the staffing of the hostels was very much a matter of concern to us.

(3) It might happen that quite suddenly a warden could not tolerate a particular child any longer, and that the objective assessment of this problem required a very intimate knowledge of the situation. We acted on the principle that a warden should be able to express his feelings to someone who could, if necessary, take action, or who could prevent the matter from developing into an unnecessary crisis.

CLASSIFICATION FOR PLACING

In different types of psychiatric work different ways of classifying patients are appropriate. For the purposes of placing these children satisfactorily in hostels, classification according to symptoms was useless, and was set aside. The following principles were developed and followed.

1. In many cases no adequate diagnosis can usefully be made till a child has been watched, in a group, over a period of time.

In regard to the length of time needed a week is better than nothing, but three months is better than a week.

2. If a history of the child's development can be obtained, the existence or non-existence of a fairly stable home is a fact of prime importance.

In the former case the child's experience of home can be used, and the hostel can remind the child of his own home and extend the existing home idea. In the latter case, the hostel has to provide a primary home, and the child's idea of his own home then gets mixed up with the ideal home of his dreams, compared with which the hostel is a pretty poor place.

3. If a home of any kind does exist, then it is important to know of abnormalities there.

Examples of these are a parent who is a psychiatric case, certified or uncertifiable, or a dominating or anti-social brother or sister, or housing conditions that are in themselves a persecution. Hostel life can offer some correction of these abnormalities in the course of time and very gradually enable the child to view his own home objectively, and even sympathetically.

4. If further details are available, it is of great importance to know whether the child did or did not have a satisfactory infant-mother relationship.

If there has been an experience of a good early relationship, even if this has been lost, it may be recovered in the personal relation of some member of the hostel staff to the child. If no such good start in fact existed it is beyond the scope of a hostel to create this, *ab initio*. The answer to this important question is often one of degree, but it is nevertheless worth seeking. In many cases a reliable early history is unobtainable, in which case the past has to be reconstructed, through observation of the child in the hostel over a period of months.

5. During the period of observation in the hostel there are certain specially valuable indications—ability to play, to persevere in constructive effort, and to make friends.

If a child can play, this is a very favourable sign. If constructive effort is enjoyed and persevered in without undue supervision and encouragement there is even greater hope of useful work being done through the hostel life. The ability to make a friend is a further valuable sign. Anxious children change friends frequently and too easily, and seriously disturbed children can only achieve membership of a gang—that is to say, a group whose cohesion depends on engineered persecution. A majority of the children drafted to evacuation hostels were at the outset incapable of play, or of sustained constructive effort, or of friendship.

6. Mental defect has obvious importance, and in any group of hostels for difficult children there should be separate accommodation for children with low intelligence.

This is not only because they need special management and education, but also because they wear out the hostel staff to no purpose, and cause a feeling of hopelessness. In such difficult work as that with problem children, there must be some hope of reward, even if reward does not actually come.

7. Bizarre or 'scatty' behaviour, and odd characteristics, distinguish some children who are on the whole unpromising material for therapy by hostel management.

Such children puzzle the hostel staffs and make them feel mad themselves. In any case children of this kind need personal psychotherapy; although, even if it can be provided, their treatment is often beyond present-day understanding. They are, in fact, research cases for enterprising analysts, and there are but few satisfactory institutions for these children.

The classification outlined above formed the basis for placing; but the main consideration must always be: what can this hostel, these wardens, this group of children, stand at this particular moment? It was soon found to be a bad thing to decide to put a child in a hostel just because he was needing care and the hostel had a vacancy. Every new child, disturbed in the way that these billet-failures were disturbed, cannot help being, at first, a complication, and no asset to a hostel community. These children (except possibly in the first deceptive and unreal week or two) contribute nothing, and they absorb emotional energy. If they become accepted in the group they then start to be able to contribute to some extent, under supervision; but this is the result of hard work on the part of staff and the established children.

There is no one thing that is more helpful to the wardens of a hostel than this: that on introducing a new child one should present that child to the wardens before the issue of placing the child is settled. If this course is followed, a child is suggested for the hostel, but the wardens can accept or refuse. If the wardens think they can absorb this new child, then they have begun to want him. By the other method, of simply drafting children without prior consultation, wardens cannot help starting with negative feelings towards the child, and can only find other feelings in the course of time, and with luck. This joint consultation over admission to a particular hostel was very difficult to put into practice, but every effort was made to avoid exceptions to the rule, because of the vast practical difference between the two methods.

THE CENTRAL THERAPEUTIC IDEA

The central idea of the scheme was to provide stability which the children could get to know, which they could test out, which they could gradually come to believe in, and around which they could play. This stability was essentially something that existed apart from the ability of the children, individually or collectively, to create or maintain it.[6]

The environmental stability was passed down, from the community in general, to the children. The Ministry provided the background, helped by the County Council. Against this background there was the committee, which in this scheme was, fortunately, made up of a group of experienced and responsible people who could be relied upon to continue to exist. Then there were the hostel staffs, as well as the buildings and grounds, and the general emotional atmosphere. It was the task of the psychiatric team to translate the essential stability of the scheme into terms of emotional stability in the hostels. Only if the wardens are happy, and satisfied, and feeling stable, can the children benefit from their relations to them. Wardens in these hostels are in so difficult a position that understanding and support from someone is an absolute necessity for them. In the scheme we are describing it was the job of the psychiatric team to supply this support.

The most essential thing, then, was the provision of stability, and especially of emotional stability, in the hostel staff; although, of course, this could never be completely achieved. Nevertheless, work was done all the time with this aim. To help in the creation of a stable emotional background for the children the policy of employing married wardens—mentioned earlier—was recommended to the committee, and adopted. Joint married wardens may have children of their own, and then immense complications ensue. Nevertheless, these complications are outweighed by the enrichment of the hostel community through the existence of a real family within it.

It was once said in criticism, 'The hostel looks as if it were made for the staff'; but we felt that this was not a criticism. The staff must be living a satisfactory life, must be allowed time off, proper holidays, and, in peacetime, proper financial reward, if work with anti-social and mad children is to be done at all. It is not enough to provide a beautiful hostel with a nice staff. To do good by residential management the staff of the hostels must 'stay put' for a period of time—long enough for them to see children through to

---

[6] Surely, experiments in getting children to create their own central government should always be made first, if they have to be made, with those who have had a good early home experience? With these deprived children it seems to be cruel to make them do the very thing they feel hopeless about.

school-leaving age, and to the age of going to work; for the work of the staff is not finished until they have gradually launched the children into the world.

I

There is no particular training for hostel wardens, and even if there were, their selection as suitable people for the work would be of more importance than their training. We find it impossible to generalise about the type of person who makes a good warden. Our successful wardens have differed from each other widely in education, previous experience, and interests, and have been drawn from various walks of life. The following is a list of the previous occupations of some of them : elementary school teacher, social worker, trained church worker, commercial artist, instructor and matron in an approved school, master and matron at a remand home, worker in a public assistance institution, prison welfare officer.

We find that the nature of previous training and experience matters little compared with the ability to assimilate experience, and to deal in a genuine, spontaneous way with the events and relationships of life. This is of the utmost importance, for only those who are confident enough to be themselves, and to act in a natural way, can act consistently day in and day out. Furthermore, wardens are put to such a severe test by the children coming into hostels that only those who are able to be themselves can stand the strain. We must point out, however, that there will be times when the warden will have to 'act naturally' in the sense that an actor acts naturally. This is particularly important with ill children. If a child comes and whines : 'I've cut my finger', just when the warden is in the middle of making Income Tax returns, or when the cook has given notice, he or she must act as though the child had not come in at such an awkward moment; for these children are often too ill or too anxious to be able to allow for the warden's own personal difficulties as well as their own.

We therefore try to choose as hostel wardens those who possess this ability to be consistently natural in their behaviour, for we regard it as essential to the work. We would count as important also the possession of some skill, such as music, painting, pottery, etc. Above and beyond all these things, however, it is, of course, vital that the wardens possess a genuine love of children, for only this will see them through the inevitable ups and downs of hostel life.

Brilliant people who organise one hostel well, and pass on to another to do the same there, would be better if they had never existed as far as the children are concerned. It is the permanent nature of the home that makes it valuable, even more than the fact that the work is done intelligently.

We do not expect the wardens to carry out any prescribed type of regime, or even to carry out agreed plans. Wardens who have to be told what to do are of no use, because the important things have to be done on the spot in a way that is natural to the individual concerned. Only thus will the warden's relationship become real and therefore of importance to the child. Wardens are encouraged to build up a home and community life to the best of their ability, and it will be found that this is along the line of their own beliefs and way of life. No two hostels will therefore be alike.

We find that there are wardens who like organising large groups of children, and others who prefer to have intimate personal relationships with a few children. Some prefer abnormal children of one type or another, and some like true mental defectives.

The education of the wardens in the work is important, and has been discussed earlier as part of the work of the psychiatrist, and of the psychiatric social worker. This education is best done on the job, by the discussion of problems as they arise. It is a great help if wardens are confident enough in themselves to be able to think along psychological lines and discuss problems with other wardens and experienced people.

The staffing of hostels apart from the wardens presents peculiar difficulties, especially where the children are rather anti-social. With normal children the assistants can be young people who are learning the job, practising taking responsibility and acting on their own initiative, with a view to becoming wardens themselves at a later date. Where the children are anti-social, however, the management has to be strong, and cannot avoid being dictatorial, so that assistants have to be constantly carrying out orders from the warden when they would prefer to be working on their own initiative. They therefore become easily bored, or else they like being told what to do, in which case they are not much good. These problems are inherent in the work.

2

If it is recognised how intimately a child's sense of security is bound up with his relationship to his parents, it becomes obvious that no other people can give him so much. Every child has the right to his own good home in which to grow, and it is nothing but a misfortune that deprives him of it.

In our hostel work, therefore, we recognise that we cannot give to the children anything so good as their own good home would have been. We can only offer a substitute home.

Each hostel tries to reproduce as nearly as possible a home environment for each child in it. This means first of all the provision of positive things : a building, food, clothing, human love and understanding; a timetable, schooling; apparatus and ideas leading to rich play and constructive work. The hostel also provides substitute parents and other human relationships. And then, these things being provided, each child, according to the degree of his distrust, and according to the degree of his hopelessness about the loss of his own home (and sometimes his recognition of the inadequacies of that home while it lasted), is all the time testing the hostel staff as he would test his own parents. Sometimes he does this directly, but most of the time he is content to let another child do the testing for him. An important thing about this testing is that it is not something that can be achieved and done with. Always somebody has to be a nuisance. Often one of the staff will say : 'We'd be all right if it weren't for Tommy . . .', but in point of fact the others can only afford to be 'all right' because Tommy is being a nuisance, and is proving to them that the home can stand up to Tommy's testing, and could therefore presumably stand up to their own.

The usual response of a child who is placed in a good hostel can be described as having three phases. For the first short phase the child is remarkably 'normal' (it will be a long time before he is so normal again); he has new hope, he scarcely sees people as they are, and the staff and the other children have not yet had any reason to begin to disillusion him. Almost every child goes through a short period of good behaviour when he first comes to a hostel. It is a dangerous stage, because what he sees and responds to in the warden and his staff is his ideal of what a good father and mother would be like. Grown-ups are inclined to think, 'This child sees we are nice, and easily trusts us.' But he does not see they are nice; he does not see *them* at all; he just imagines they are nice. It is a symptom of illness to believe that anything can be 100 per cent good, and the child starts off with an ideal which is destined to be shattered.

The child sooner or later enters into the second phase, the breaking down of his ideal. He sets about this first by testing the building and the people physically. He wants to know what damage he can do, and how much he can do with impunity. Then if he finds that he can be physically managed, that is, that the place and the people in it have nothing to fear from him physically, he starts to test by subtlety, putting one member of the staff against another, trying to make people quarrel, trying to make people give each other away, and doing all he can to get favoured himself. When a hostel is being managed unsatisfactorily it is this second phase which becomes almost a constant feature.

If the hostel withstands these tests the child enters on the third phase, settles down with a sigh of relief, and joins in the life of the group as an ordinary member. It should be borne in mind that his first real contacts with the other children will probably be in the shape of a fight or some kind of attack, and we have noticed that often the first child to be attacked by a new child will later become that child's first friend.

In short, the hostels provide positive good things, and give opportunities for their value and reality to be tested continuously by the children. Sentimentality has no place in the management of children, and no ultimate good can come from offering children artificial conditions of indulgence; by carefully administered justice they must gradually be brought up against the consequences of their own destructive actions. Each child will be able to stand this in so far as he has been able to get some positive good out of hostel life, that is, in so far as he has found people who are truly reliable, and has begun to build up belief in them and in himself.

It must be remembered that the preservation of law and order is necessary to the children, and will be a relief to them, for it means that the hostel life and the good things for which the hostel stands will be preserved in spite of all that they can do.

The immense strain of the twenty-four-hour care of these children is not easily recognised in high quarters, and in fact any one who is only visiting a hostel, and who is not emotionally involved, can easily forget this fact. It might be asked why the wardens should let themselves get emotionally involved. The answer is that these children, who are seeking a primary home experience, do not get anywhere unless someone does, in fact, get emotionally involved with them. To get under someone's skin is the first thing these children do, when they begin to get hope. The experience subsequent to this state forms the essence of hostel therapeutics.

It follows, therefore, that hostels must be small. Moreover, wardens must not be burdened with one more child than they can emotionally stand at any given moment: for if one too many is put in a warden's care he is forced to protect himself, by ousting from 'under his skin' someone who is not ready for this. There is a limit to the number of people that a human being can be seriously concerned with at one time, and if this fact is ignored the warden is forced to do superficial and useless work, and to substitute dictatorial management for the healthy mixture of love and strength which he would prefer to show. Alternatively, and this is common, he breaks down, and the work he has done is undone. For every change of wardens produces casualties among the children, and interrupts the natural therapeutics of hostel work.

7

Children's Hostels in War and Peace[1]

[1948]

EVACUATION produced its own problems and wartime its own
solutions to problems. Can we make use, in peace, of the
results of what was so painfully experienced in time of acute
stress and awareness of common danger?

Probably very little that was new in psychological theory came
out of the evacuation experience, but there is little doubt that
because of it things became known to very large numbers of people
who would otherwise have remained ignorant. Especially did the
general public become aware of the fact of anti-social behaviour,
from bed-wetting to train-wrecking.

It has been truly said that the fact of anti-social behaviour is in
itself a stabilising factor in society, it is (in one way of speaking) a
return of the repressed, a reminder of individual spontaneity or
impulsiveness, and of society's denial of the unconscious to which
instinct is relegated.

For my part, I was fortunate in being employed by a county
council (from 1939 to 1946) in connection with a group of five
hostels for children who were difficult to billet. In the course of this
work,[2] which involved a visit each week to the county, I had
detailed knowledge of 285 children, most of whom were observed

[1] A contribution to the symposium on 'Lessons for Child Psychiatry' given at
a meeting of the medical section of the British Psychological Society on
February 27, 1946.
[2] A description of this work from different angles can be read in: (a) Winnicott & Britton, 'The Problems of Homeless Children', *New Education Fellow-
ship Monograph*, 1944, no. 1, p. 1; (b) Winnicott & Britton, 'Residential
Management as Treatment for Difficult Children: The Evolution of a Wartime Hostels Scheme', *Human Relations*, 1947, vol. 1, no. 1, p. 87. These two
papers have been dovetailed together to form Chapter 6 of this section.

over a period of years. Our job was to cope with the immediate problem and we succeeded or failed in so far as we did or did not relieve those in charge of the local evacuation arrangements of difficulties which threatened the success of their work. Now the war is over, there is still some value to be got out of the experience we went through, especially out of this fact of the public's new awareness of anti-social tendencies as psychological phenomena.

Of course, we must avoid seeming to suggest that hostels (or boarding-schools for maladjusted children, as they are officially called now) are a panacea for emotional disturbance of children. We tend to think of hostel management simply because the alternative is merely to do nothing at all through the shortage of psychotherapists. But this tendency has to be checked. With this proviso it can be said that there are children who urgently need to be cared for in some kind of home. In my clinic at the Paddington Green Children's Hospital (a medical out-patient department) there is a proportion of cases absolutely needing hostel management.

There are two broad categories of such children in peace time : children whose homes do not exist or whose parents cannot form a stable background in which a child can develop, and children with an existing home which, nevertheless, contains a mentally ill parent. Such children appear in our peacetime clinics, and we find they need just what the children who were difficult to billet needed. Their home environment has failed them. Let us say that what these children need is *environmental stability, personal* management, and *continuity* of management. We assume an ordinary standard of physical care.

To ensure personal management the staffing of a hostel must be adequate, and the wardens must be able to stand the emotional strain that belongs to the proper care of any child, but especially to the care of children whose own homes have failed to bear such strain. Because of this the wardens need constant support from psychiatrist and psychiatric social worker.[3] The children (unselfconsciously) look to the hostel, or failing that to society in a wider sense, to provide the framework for their lives that their own homes

[3] It would seem to be the psychiatrist's job to be to some extent responsible for the staffing because the mental and physical state of the staff is the main thing in the therapy. A hostel whose staff is appointed and managed by one authority and whose children are under the care of another is unlikely to be successful.

have failed to give them. Inadequate staffing not only makes personal management impossible, but also it leads to ill-health and breakdowns in the staff, and therefore interferes with continuity of personal relationship, which is essential in this work.

A psychiatrist who is in charge of a clinic from which cases are referred to hostels should be responsible for a hostel himself, so that he may keep in touch with the special problems involved in such work. The same is true of magistrates at juvenile courts, who would do well to sit on hostel committees.

Psychotherapy. In dealing with anti-social children in clinics it is useless just to recommend psychotherapy. The first essential is to get each child properly placed, and proper placing in itself works as a therapy in a fair proportion of cases, given time. Psychotherapy can be added. It is essential to get the therapy arranged tactfully. If a psychotherapist is available, and if the hostel wardens actually want to help with regard to a child, then individual psychotherapy can be added. But there is a complication which cannot be ignored; in the good care of a child of this type the child has to become almost a part of the warden, and if someone else is giving treatment the child is apt to lose something vital in his relation to the warden (or some member of the staff), and the psychotherapist cannot easily make up for this in spite of the fact that he can give deeper understanding. Wardens, if they are good at this special type of job, must tend to dislike psychotherapy of the children in their care. In the same way good parents hate their children to be undergoing analysis, even when they seek it and co-operate fully.

The psychiatric social worker and myself, in this scheme, kept in intimate contact with the wardens both in regard to their personal problems, and to the children and the problems of their management as they arose. This contrasts with ordinary clinic work in which the psychiatrist can do best in a direct personal relation to each child patient, and to the parents.

Provision of hostels. We must not be surprised to find ministries issuing edicts in favour of hostels, and also to meet children in need of hostels, and yet to find nothing happening, even to find hostels everywhere closing down. The contact between the supply and the need is only to be provided by men and women who are able and willing to live an experience with the children, willing to let a group steal a few years of their lives. Those of us who are clinically

I

involved with these children must all the time play a part in bringing together the three things—official policy, wardens, and children— and must not expect anything good really to happen apart from our own personal voluntary deliberate efforts. Even in State Medicine the ideas and the clinical contacts belong to the clinician, without whom the best scheme is void.

Placing. The obvious method to be adopted by a large body (such as the London County Council, or a ministry) is to work the distribution of cases from a central bureau which keeps in touch with the various groups of hostels. If I have a child in my clinic needing a hostel (and it is always urgent), I am to send a report including Intelligence Quotient and school report to the central bureau, from which each case is to be distributed according to routine. But I do not play the game, nor do the parents, except when the child is so awful that the only need is to be rid of him immediately. In this mass-production arrangement something personal is lacking. The fact is that if a child comes under my care I cannot just put his or her name on a list somewhere. Doctors and parents must be allowed to maintain interest in the placing of their children ; they must actually find out that what is provided is good.

There must be some personal link between clinic and hostel ; someone must know someone. If no one knows any one then suspicion develops, because *in the imagination* there are bad parents, bad doctors, bad wardens, bad hostels, even bad ministries. And by bad I mean malicious. If a doctor or a hostel warden is not known as good, he is easily felt to be malevolent.

It will be apparent that our convalescent homes are unsuitable for these children, usually physically healthy, who need long-term management by specially chosen wardens supported by the psychiatric social worker and psychiatrist. Moreover, hospital-trained nurses seem to be rendered unsuitable for this work by their professional training ; and many paediatricians turn a blind eye to psychology.

Prevention of delinquency. This work is prophylactic work for the Home Office, whose main job it is to implement the law. For some reason or other I have met opposition to this idea from doctors who work for the Home Office. But hostels for evacuees all over the country succeeded in preventing many children from reaching the courts, thereby saving immense sums of money as well as producing citizens instead of habitual offenders; and from our point of view as doctors, the important things is that the children have been under the Ministry of Health, that is, they have been recognised as ill. One can only hope that the Ministry of Education, which is now taking over (written in 1945) will do as well during peacetime as the Ministry of Health did during the war, in this prophylactic work for the Home Office.

Main thesis. It happened that by my two appointments I was in touch with the London need for hostels at the same time as I was involved in the provision of hostels in an evacuation area. As physician to a London children's hospital, I was struck by the way in which this wartime provision solved the peacetime problem of management of the early anti-social case.

In sixteen instances I was able to draft London out-patient children to the hostels which I was visiting as psychiatrist. It came about by the chance that I held the two appointments, and it seemed to me to be a good arrangement, one that could be adapted to peace conditions. Because of my position I could be the link between the child, the parents or relatives, and the hostel wardens, and also between the child's past, present, and future.

The value of this work is not to be assessed only by the degree of relief of the psychiatric illness of each child. The value lies also in the provision of a place where the physician could care for these children who, without such provision, must degenerate at hospital or at home, causing great distress to adults, and badly affecting other children.

It is a sad reflection that many of the wartime hostels have closed down, and now there is no serious attempt to provide the hostel accommodation urgently needed for the early anti-social case. As for mad children, for them there is practically no provision. Officially, they do not exist.

PART III

Reflections on Impulse in Children

1

Towards an Objective Study of Human Nature[1]

[1945]

Y ou have invited me to speak to you on the subject of the background of psychology, its basic assumptions and discoveries. In order not to get lost in so large a subject, I must speak of the small part of it which comes my way; or, shall I say, I must be allowed to look at the whole from my particular angle.

I shall not be able to do what I ought to do, which is to take into consideration the fact that you yourselves who are listening to me come to the subject each from your own direction. Some of you think easily in terms of scientific experiment, others are used to being taught the facts, in so far as they are known, of history or geography; and among you there are some with strong intuitive bent, who like to approach any new subject subjectively at first, having ideas which you are unwilling to develop until you have stated them and recognised them as your own. I cannot cater for all this, so I shall go at it my own way.

I want to put before you the view that psychology simply means the study of human nature, and that it is a science, just as physics, physiology, and biology are sciences. This is my view, and my life's work is based on this assumption, for I think you ought to know at the outset that I am not only a doctor but also a psycho-analyst.

Psycho-analysis has only recently become recognised as a serious subject. As a word it has now passed into common speech and, as usual when this happens, it has come to mean something different

[1] Being a lecture given, by invitation of the High Master, to the Eighth Form of St. Paul's School, London, 1945. I wish to thank my colleague Mr. Masud Khan for advice leading to modifications of the original lecture.

when used popularly from what it means technically. If you were to ask a doctor just what part psycho-analysis is playing now in the general medical field, and in the whole study of human nature, you would be unlikely to get correct information. The tendency to examine the psychological factors of every case that can be found in medicine to-day is extremely new, and it will take a generation more before the work that has already been done by psycho-analysis will be fully applied in ordinary medical practice. Some of you will become doctors, and a few will probably wish to practise in that part of doctoring which particularly involves the study of the mind, and then you will need, in addition to the ordinary medical training, a training in the psycho-analytic technique; but you can be helped by such training even if you plan to do that most difficult of all medical jobs, to be a good family general practitioner.

Psychology makes no claim to priority in regard to the understanding of human nature, except in one respect, that is to say, in the making of this study a science. For instance, it is possible that everything that can be discovered by psycho-analysis can be shown to have been understood by Shakespeare, taking Shakespeare as a good example of someone with intuitive understanding, based, of course, on observation as well as on feeling or empathy. Each step forward that we make in the science of psychology enables us to see more in Shakespeare's plays, just as it enables us to talk less foolishly about human nature. Talk we must, and psychology as a science justifies itself, in my opinion, if it enables us to talk less foolishly.

Also, it is not suggested that no psychological healing took place before psycho-analysis came on the field. Good doctors have always been good psychologists in so far as they could *feel* the patient's position in his relation to external reality and also in his relation to his private inner world. But doctors when they *talk* about human nature, say silly things just as other people do. Intuitive understanding of human nature must often prove unreliable as a guide in the more general field of social living. It might enable a doctor to be brilliantly understanding of a patient who was a thief, but unless the psychology of delinquency is studied as a science, intuitive understanding will not prevent doctors as well as other people from doing and saying all sorts of useless things when decisions have to be taken in a practical way, as, for instance, in a juvenile court.

The doctor's long and arduous training does nothing to qualify him in psychology, and does much to disqualify him; it keeps him so busy from 18 to 25 that he finds he is middle-aged before he has the leisure in which to discover himself. It takes him years of medical practice, and a struggle to find time to live his own life, before he can catch up on his fellow creatures, many of whom have lived a lot by the time they are 25.

Perhaps you are beginning to see that there is some point in making the study of human nature a science, a process characterised by observation of facts, by the building of theory and the testing of it, and by modification of theory according to the discovery of new facts. Can you see the one essential way in which science and intuition contrast with each other? True intuition can reach to a whole truth in a flash (just as faulty intuition can reach to error), whereas in a science the whole truth is never reached. What is important in science is a construction of a satisfactory road towards the truth. That is why a scientific training is so important for everybody; it enables you and me to test our own little bits of the world satisfactorily. Our feelings and our imaginings may get out of hand and may take us anywhere, this moment enabling us to dream we are able to fly and the next moment allowing us to feel infinitely unsupported, so that we fall and fall, and there is no bottom, except waking, which means a return to science, to the well-tested and welcome external reality.

Have you ever thought of science just in this way? If, in a subject that is being approached through the scientific method, there is a gap in our knowledge, we just record it as a gap in knowledge, a stimulus to research, but the intuitive person's gaps are unknown quantities with somewhat terrifying potential. The physicists say that there is an element that we have not yet discovered. No one gets in a panic; later on the new element is found, and it fits into the scheme of things. When the drug M and B was discovered no one knew why it acted in the way it did act, but no one suggested that its action was anything to do with magic; the biochemists simply felt stimulated by the fact of their ignorance, and they gradually found out more and more, but they still do not know all they want to know about it. In psychology there are many huge gaps in our knowledge. But, since psychology is a science, we do not even mind when the intuitive people say of something we have discovered, 'We have always known that'; for they do not mention at the same time all the weird things they also knew, wrongly. The scientific approach to the phenomena of human nature enables us to be ignorant without being frightened, and without, therefore, having to invent all sorts of weird theories to explain away the gaps in knowledge.

You and I started as scientists when we were very young, in fact as soon as we were born. We started life as scientists provided we had good enough mothering in the very early stages, so that we did not get pushed into a muddle. We were then at the mercy of our imaginings, and, as soon as we could perceive external reality, every real thing happening to us was welcome as depending on something external to ourselves, and therefore dependable, because of being something we could get to know. Even things that made us angry, like being kept waiting when we were hungry, had a value for us. External reality helped us to stand the magic quality of our ideas, which at that time were very primitive because we had so little experience of real things, and so we had nothing to dream about, only (one might say) feelings to feel. These magical primitive feelings can be indeed very alarming as well as wonderful, as we see from the study of those people who have not succeeded in coming to terms with them, and who are insane. Many people develop a scientific interest in external reality to get away from the intuitive and the subjective approach to life. I suppose Western culture, on the whole, tends towards an exclusion of *feelings* by scientific *thinking,* whereas in Eastern culture the scientific method is relatively despised. In the best of our Western culture we enjoy a scientific method of approach to external reality—whilst at the same time we preserve in music, painting, and poetry, and in religion, the recognition of the importance of the creative and intuitive approach to life, as well as the magic of primitive feeling and spontaneous instinctual expression.

Well, if we agree to all that, why not settle down to the scientific study of human nature? Why has psychology come at the end of the sciences, following biology, which, I suppose, could be said, in one sense, to have followed physics? (Of course, I know they co-exist to-day.)

Obviously the more closely connected a science is with life the more difficult it is for a scientific approach to seem adequate. I remember my excitement in my own schooldays before the First World War when I first met Darwin's *Origin of Species*. I could not leave off reading it.

'Then felt I like some watcher of the skies
　　When a new planet swims into his ken;
　　Or like stout Cortez . . .'

At the time I did not quite know why it was so important to me, but I see now that the main thing was that it showed that living things could be examined scientifically, with the corollary that gaps in knowledge and understanding need not scare me. For me this new idea meant a great lessening of tension and consequently a release of energy for work and play.

I feel sure that if I were at school now I should find the same value in the corresponding book that would put psychology on the map as a science, but I think there is no book exactly corresponding to the *Origin of Species*. No doubt the latter would be said now to contain many fallacies and misstatements, but the same could even more strongly be said of any one book dealing with psychology. Freud's *Introductory Lectures* might be cited. There have been such tremendous advances, many of them Freud's own, since Freud wrote this pioneer work, that a psycho-analyst might well hesitate before recommending even that one book, except to be read along with many others, and read with full knowledge that Freud was starting a new science. Freud's works, read in chronological order, give a good picture of the way his ideas developed. He not only started a new science, but he also carried it a long way; and it is now being carried further by those who have continued to use his methods, and to develop them in their own ways.

Now let me say something about the difficulties inherent in the science of psychology. I shall begin by quoting what I said just now. I said that a scientific training was important because it enabled us to test our own little bit of the world satisfactorily. When it comes to psychology these words 'our own little bit of the world' mean not only the phenomena of other people's human nature but also our own. In this respect psychology is distinct from other sciences and must always remain so. With our minds we are examining the very minds we are using, and with our feelings we are examining our feelings. It is like trying to examine a microscope under its own high power. No wonder psychology came last in the sequence of sciences. Many people hold the view that psychology can never be a science because of this difficulty, and the impasse of (so-called) academic psychology illustrates the dilemma, but Freud went ahead in spite of this, and some of us think that he had already established psychology as a science at the beginning of this century. In *The Interpretation of Dreams* you will see how he showed that what most people regard as an insuperable barrier to psychology as a science could actually be turned to use in furthering scientific investigation. He realised that if he were to claim that he could use his patients' dreams, believing in the significance of every detail recorded by the dreamer, he must show willingness and ability to examine his own dreams. Most of what Freud said about dreams was original and brilliantly constructive, and has stood the test of time. *The Psychopathology of Everyday Life* was another book in which he started to put before the public the possibility of a science of psychology, and there was a steady stream of scientific work from this great man. I was unaware when I was at school that these books were already written, and I doubt if I was ready for them then.

I now come to the main difficulty of psychology as a science, and there Freud made his most important discovery. In no other science is there a twist corresponding to that produced in psychology by the existence of the unconscious. The word 'unconscious' can, of course, mean the sort of thing that happens when you get a crack on the head and pass out. Psychologically the word has other meanings, and it has been used for a very long time to describe unawareness. For instance, one cannot, at any one moment in time, be aware of everything that one could theoretically be aware of. In painting, an artist may reach feelings of which he was unaware before he started, and which may come from so deep in his nature that he is hard put to it to acknowledge responsibility for his picture.

Freud was not daunted by the well-known fact that there are depths to our natures which we cannot easily plumb. He discovered and established by scientific method that there is a special variety of unconscious, which he named the *repressed unconscious;* here the trouble is not the depth of the thing of which the individual is unaware, but the fact that what is unconscious cannot be remembered because of its being associated with painful feeling or some other intolerable emotion. Energy has to be all the time employed in maintaining the repression, and it can easily be seen that if there is a great deal of an individual's personality that is repressed there is relatively little energy left for a direct participation in life. The first reason why people can get practical help from psycho-analytic treatment is that in so far as it is successful, it enables the patient to release painful material from repression, with the consequence that the patient has all that energy which formerly was used in the service of repression for the enjoyment of life and for constructive being.

Freud invented and developed a method, an instrument of scientific research into human nature which has turned out to be, at the same time, a method of treatment. Briefly described, psycho-analysis is: that the psycho-analyst prepares stable and simplified conditions in which the individual who undergoes psycho-analysis can let his mind work freely. Sooner or later he will be found to be approaching the difficult part of himself, showing in his relation to the analyst that he is wanting to relive even the episodes and types of emotional experience which for him are associated with so much pain that he is not able to reach them on his own. Thus growth that was held up can take place.

In the simplest possible example, a person who is being analysed is able to correct a past experience, or an imaginary experience, by reliving it in simplified conditions in which the pain can be tolerated because of its being spread over a period of time, taken, so to speak, in small doses, in a controlled emotional environment. As you can well imagine, in actual practice there is seldom anything as uncomplicated as this, but the main thing can legitimately be described in this way.

In a psycho-analytic treatment the analyst and the person being analysed are working together on a problem on equal terms. This makes the psycho-analytic method applicable to the treatment of many people who would not allow themselves to be totally in the power of another individual, even for a short period, as in treatment by hypnotism, even though by hypnotism it might be easier for a doctor to effect removal of symptoms. Freud's invention, psycho-analysis, was more important than a mere treatment, for its aim was not primarily the removal of symptoms; its aim was a scientific one: to approach a little bit of truth for the sake of truth itself. Undoubtedly, one of the early good effects of the process is an indirect one, due to the fact that the person being analysed begins to feel that emotional phenomena *can* be examined scientifically so that all the enormous gaps in his understanding of himself become just so many things not yet understood, instead of sources of anxiety and invitations for the construction of false theories and philoso phies.

You will readily see that one important consequence of all this is that psycho-analysis rescues logic from the death to which it was fast sinking after a brilliant start. We can see now what was wrong with logic, and why it lacked social usefulness when it should have been able to make human behaviour more calculable and so strengthen the roots of society. It quickly got as far as it could ever get without taking into account the unconscious to which Freud introduced us, the repressed unconscious, the part of the personality of which the individual cannot become aware, and against aware ness of which he must defend himself with all his power and skill

Through psycho-analysis, insight is being gained into the causes of much that is unhealthy in persons and in society. At the same time through psycho-analysis there has come about an increased understanding of the development of man's conscience, and also of his constructive or sublimatory potential, looked at as a compromise between instinctual drives and the demands of a mature and personal conscience. The compromise enables the individual to harness instinctual energy in a way that does not violate his relation to the social structure.

Incidentally, when investigation into neurosis is made, it is always found that the blockage holding up emotional development has its origin in early childhood. It is at about the years of 2, 3, and 4, when the most intense interpersonal relationships are being experi enced, that the most severe anxiety is roused. Anxiety leads to a setting up of defences in the individual and it is these organised defences that appear as neurotic illness or character disturbances. At this time when the child is 2, 3, or 4 years old, the individual is not yet an independent unit; at this age in a child the Ego can be said to be in the process of building up a personal Super-ego for the management and employment of the Id (instincts). Loving human beings and a stable environment are particularly necessary during this period, and the people around are used by the growing child as ideals, and as strict persons, during the process of the construction in the individual of the more personal Super-ego, with its own ideas about control and licence. This is a statement in psycho-analytic terms; the terms of course are not essential, but they are useful symbols for theoretical construction and for discussion.

The more and more profound disorders that are usually known as the psychoses have their origin earlier and earlier in infancy, in the period in which the personality is not yet integrated into a unit, and when the capacity for communication with external reality is tenuous and not yet established.

Thus psycho-analysis turns out to be a fine new instrument by which human beings may study themselves and their interpersonal relationships; but it does remain an instrument of scientific research or a therapy, and it never makes a direct philosophical or a religious contribution. Freud took pains to point this out, and those who come to psycho-analysis for the first time will do well to be quite clear about the limitations of its aims and aspirations.

There is one thing that could be added. People often ask whether psycho-analysis makes life easy. Quite naturally they would suspect anything which made such a claim. Psycho-analysis, apart from its being a painful process in itself, does not alter the fact that life is difficult. The best that can happen is that the person who is being analysed gradually comes to feel less and less at the mercy of unknown forces both within and without, and more and more able to deal in his or her own peculiar way with the difficulties inherent in human nature, in personal growth, and in the gradual achieve-ment of a mature and constructive relationship to society.

2

Further Thoughts on Babies as Persons

[1947]

THE human being's development is a continuous process. As in the development of the body, so in development of the personality and in the development of the capacity for relationships. No stage can be missed or marred without ill-effect.

Health is maturity, maturity appropriate to the age. If certain accidental diseases are ignored this is obviously true of the body, and in matters of psychology there are practically no reasons why health and maturity should not mean the same thing. In other words, in the emotional development of a human being, if there are no hitches or distortions in the developmental process, there is health.

This means, if I am right, that all the care that a mother and father take of their infant is not just a pleasure to them and to the infant, it is also absolutely necessary, and without it the baby cannot easily grow up into a healthy or valuable adult.

In matters of the body it is possible to make mistakes, even to allow rickets, and yet rear a child with nothing worse than bow-legs. But on the psychological side, a baby deprived of some quite ordinary but necessary thing, such as affectionate contact, is bound, to some extent, to be disturbed in emotional development, and this will show in a personal difficulty as the young person grows up. Put the other way round; as a child develops and passes from stage to stage of complex internal development and the development of capacity for relationships, the parents can know that their good care has been an essential ingredient. This has a meaning for us all, for it follows that, in so far as we are reasonably mature or healthy as adults, each one of us must recognise that a good start to one's life was provided by someone. It is this good start—this basis for child care—that I try to describe.

The story of a human being does not start at 5 years or 2, or at six months, but starts at birth—and before birth if you like; and each baby is from the start a person, and needs to be known by someone. No one can get to know a baby as well as the baby's own mother.

These two statements take us a long way, but now, how to proceed? Can psychology tell any one how to be a mother or father? I think this is the wrong way round. Let us, instead, study some of the things mothers and fathers naturally do, and try to show them a little why they do them, so that they may feel strengthened.

I will take an example.

Here is a mother with her baby girl. What does she do when she picks her up? Does she catch hold of her foot and drag her out of her pram and swing her up? Does she hold a cigarette with one hand and grab her with the other? No. She has quite a different way of going at it. I think she tends to give the infant warning of her approach, she puts her hands round her to gather her together before she moves her; in fact she gains the baby's co-operation before she lifts her; and then she lifts her from one place to another, from cot to shoulder. Does she not then put the baby up against her with her head snuggled in her neck, so that the baby may begin to feel her as a person?

Here is a mother with her baby boy. How does she bath him? Does she just put him in the electric washer and let the cleaning process happen mechanically? Not at all. She knows of bath-time as a special time both for her and for the baby. She prepares to enjoy it. She does all the mechanical part properly, testing the heat of the water with her elbow and not letting the baby slip through her fingers when he is soapy, but on top of this she allows the bathing to be an enjoyed experience which enriches the growing relationship, not only of herself to the baby, but of him to her.

Why does she take all this trouble? Can we not say quite simply, and without being sentimental, that it is because of love; that it is because maternal feelings have developed in her; because of the deep understanding of her baby's needs that comes from her devotion?

Let us go back to the business of picking a baby up. Can we not say that, without conscious effort, the mother did what she did in stages. She made being picked up acceptable to her little girl by :

(1) giving the infant warning ;
(2) gaining her co-operation ;
(3) gathering her together ;
(4) taking her from one place to another and with a simple purpose that she can understand.

The mother also refrains from shocking her baby with cold hands or from pricking him when she pins up the napkin.

The mother does not involve her baby in all her personal experiences and feelings. Sometimes her baby yells and yells until she feels like murder, yet she lifts the baby up with just the same care, without revenge—or not very much. She avoids making the baby the victim of her own impulsiveness. Infant care, like doctoring, is a test of personal reliability.

To-day may be one of those days when everything goes wrong. The laundry man calls before the list is ready; the front door bell rings, and someone else comes to the back door. But a mother waits till she has recovered her poise before she takes up her baby, which she does with the usual gentle technique that the baby comes to know as an important part of her. Her technique is highly personal, and is looked for and recognised, like her mouth, and her eyes, her colouring, and her smell. Over and over again a mother deals with her own moods, anxieties, and excitements in her own private life, reserving for her baby what belongs to the baby. This gives a foundation on which the human infant can start to build an understanding of the extremely complex thing that is a relationship between two human beings.

Can we not say that the mother *adapts herself* to what baby can understand, actively adapts to needs ? This active adaptation is just what is essential for the infant's emotional growth, and the mother adapts herself to the baby's needs especially at the beginning, at a time when only the simplest possible circumstances can be appreciated.

I must try to explain a little why it is that a mother takes all this trouble, and so much more than I can include in this brief description. One reason why I must do this is that an important group in the present-day psychological (even psycho-analytical) world honestly believes, and is teaching, that in the first six months the mother does not matter. In the first six months (it is said) only technique counts, and a good technique can be provided in a hospital or a home, by trained workers.

For my part I am sure that while mothercraft may be taught and even read about in books, *the mothering of one's own baby is entirely personal, a job that no one else could take over and do as well.* While the scientists are at the problem, seeking proofs as they must do before believing, mothers will do well to insist that they themselves are needed from the start. My opinion, I may as well add, is not based on hearing mothers talk, on guess-work, or on pure intuition; it is the conclusion I feel I have been forced to draw after long research.

The mother takes trouble because she feels (and I find she is correct in this feeling), that if the human baby is to develop well and to develop richly, there should be personal mothering from the start, if possible by the very person who has conceived and carried that baby, the one who has a very deeply rooted interest in allowing for that baby's point of view, and who loves to let herself be the baby's whole world.

This does not mean that a baby of a few weeks knows the mother as at six months or a year. In the very first days it is the pattern and technique of mothering that is perceived, and so also the detail of her nipples, the shape of her ear, the quality of her smile, the warmth and smell of her breath. Quite early an infant may have a rudimentary idea of a kind of wholeness of the mother at certain special moments. Apart from what can be perceived, however, the infant needs the mother to be continuously there as a whole person, for only as a whole and mature human being can she have the love and character required for the task.

I once risked the remark, 'There is no such thing as a baby'—meaning that if you set out to describe a baby, you will find you are describing a *baby and someone*. A baby cannot exist alone, but is essentially part of a relationship.

The mother, too, has to be considered. If the continuity of her relationship to her own baby is broken something is lost that cannot be regained. It shows incredible lack of understanding of the mother's role to take away her baby for a few weeks, then to hand the baby back, and expect the mother to continue just where she left off.

Classification of Needs

I will try to classify some ways in which a mother is needed.

(a) First I want to say that the mother is needed as a live person. Baby must be able to feel the warmth of her skin and breath, and to taste and see. This is vitally important. There must be full access to the mother's live body. Without the mother's live presence the most learned mothercraft is wasted. It is the same with doctors. The value of a general practitioner in a village is largely that he is alive, that he is there and available. People know the number of his car, and the back view of his hat. It takes years to learn to be a doctor, the training may absorb all of a father's capital; but in the end the really important thing is not the doctor's learning and skill, but the fact that the village knows and feels that he is alive and available. The doctor's physical presence meets an emotional need. As with doctor so with mother, only much more so.

Psychology and physical care join here. During the war I was with a group of people who were discussing the future of the war-stricken children of Europe. They asked me for my opinion as to the most important *psychological* things to be done for these children at the end of the war. I found myself saying, 'Give them food.' Someone said, 'We don't mean physical things, we mean psychological things.' I still felt that the giving of food at the right moment would be catering for psychological need. Fundamentally, love expresses itself in physical terms.

Of course, if physical care means having a baby vaccinated, this has nothing to do with psychology. A baby cannot appreciate your concern lest smallpox should become rampant in the community— though the doctor's attack on his skin may of course produce crying. But if physical care means the right kind of meal at the right temperature at the right time (right from the baby's point of view, I mean), then this is psychological care too. I think this is a useful rule. The care that a baby can appreciate is fulfilling psychological and emotional needs, however much it may seem to be related simply to physical needs.

In this first way of looking at things the mother's aliveness and physical management provide an essential psychological and emotional milieu, essential for the baby's early emotional growth.

(b) Secondly, mother is needed to present the world to the baby. Through the techniques of the person or the techniques of the people who are doing the minding comes the baby's introduction to external reality, to the world around. There will continue a struggle with this difficult matter all through life, but help is needed here especially at the start. I will explain what I mean with some care, because many mothers may never have thought of infant feeding in this way; certainly doctors and nurses seldom seem to consider this aspect of the feeding act. This is what I mean.

Imagine a baby who has never had a feed. Hunger turns up, and the baby is ready to conceive of something; out of need the baby is ready to create a source of satisfaction, but there is no previous experience to show the baby what there is to expect. If at this moment the mother places her breast where the baby is ready to expect something, and if plenty of time is allowed for the infant to feel round, with mouth and hands, and perhaps with a sense of smell, the baby 'creates' just what is there to be found. The baby eventually gets the illusion that this real breast is exactly the thing that was created out of need, greed, and the first impulses of primitive loving. Sight, smell, and taste register somewhere, and after a while the baby may be creating something like the very breast that mother has to offer. A thousand times before weaning a baby may be given just this particular introduction to external reality by one woman, the mother. A thousand times the feeling has existed that what was wanted was created, and was found to be there. From this develops a belief that the world can contain what is wanted and needed, with the result that the baby has hope that there is a live relationship between inner reality and external reality, between innate primary creativity and the world at large which is shared by all.

Successful infant feeding, therefore, is an essential part of the infant's education. In the same way, but I will not try to develop the theme here, the infant needs the mother's way of receiving the excretions. The infant needs the mother's acceptance of a relationship expressed in excretion terms, a relationship that is in full swing long before the infant can contribute by conscious effort, and before the infant can (perhaps at three, four, or six months) start to wish to give to the mother out of a sense of guilt; that is to say, to make reparation for greedy attack.

(c) Out of all that could be said I will add a third way in which the mother is needed, the mother herself, and not a team of excellent minders. I refer to the mother's job of *disillusionment*. When she has given her baby the illusion that the world can be created out of need and imagination (which of course in one sense it cannot be, but we can leave this to the philosopher), when she has established the belief in things and people that I have described as a healthy basis for development, she will then have to take the child through the process of disillusionment, which is a wider aspect of weaning. The nearest that can be offered to the child is the grown-ups' *wish* to make the demands of reality bearable until the full blast of disillusionment can be borne, and until creativity can develop through mature skill into a true contribution to society.

The 'shades of the prison house' seems to me to be the poet's description of the disillusioning process, and its essential painfulness. Gradually the mother enables the child to allow that though the world *can* provide something like what is needed and wanted, and what could therefore be created, it will not do so automatically, nor at the very moment the mood arises or the wish is felt.

Do you notice how I am gradually switching from the idea of need to that of a wish or desire? The change indicates a growing up, and an acceptance of external reality with a consequent weakening of instinctual imperative.

Temporarily the mother has put herself out for the child, she has at the beginning put herself in the child's pocket. But, eventually, this child becomes able to leave the dependence that belongs to the earliest stage when the environment must adapt itself, and can accept two co-existing points of view—the mother's as well as the baby's. But the mother cannot deprive the child of herself (weaning, disillusionment) unless she has first meant everything to the child.

It is not my intention to say that the baby's whole life is wrecked if there has been a failure actually at the *breast*. Of course a baby can thrive physically on the bottle given with reasonable skill, and a mother whose breast milk fails can do almost all that is needed in the course of bottle-feeding. Nevertheless, the principle holds that a baby's emotional development at the start is only to be built well on a relationship with one person, who should, ideally, be the mother. Who else will both feel and supply what is needed?

3

Breast Feeding

[Revised in 1954]

I n a recent discussion among children's doctors it was pointed out that we do not actually know what is the particular value of breast feeding. Nor do we know what principle should govern us in our choice of the time to wean. Obviously both physiology and psychology have a place in the answering of these questions. We must leave to the pædiatricians the very complex study of the bodily processes while attempting to make a comment from the point of view of psychology.

Although the psychology of breast feeding is an extremely complex matter probably enough is already known for something clear and helpful to be written. But there is a complication. What is written is not necessarily acceptable, even if it is true. This paradox must first be dealt with.

It is not possible for an adult or even for a child to know just what it feels like to be an infant. The feelings of infancy, although no doubt stored up somewhere in every one, are not easily recaptured. The intensity of infant feelings recurs in the intensity of the suffering associated with psychotic symptoms. The infant's preoccupation with feelings of a certain type, at a certain moment, reappears in the ill person's preoccupation with fear or grief. When we observe an infant directly we find it difficult to translate what we see and hear into terms of feeling; or else we imagine, and as likely as not imagine wrongly, because we bring to the situation all sorts of ideas that belong to later development. Mothers who are caring for their own infants come nearest to a true appreciation of infant feelings because of their special ability, which they lose after a few months, to be identified with the infant that is in their special care. But mothers are seldom wanting to communicate what they know until they have forgotten the vital parts of the story.

Doctors and nurses, who are skilled in their own job, are certainly not better than other people at knowing what infants are like as human beings only just launched on the immense task of becoming themselves. It is said that there is nothing in human relationships that is more powerful than the bond between a baby and the mother (or the breast) during the excitement of a breast-feeding experience. I cannot expect this to be easily believed; nevertheless it is necessary at least to have the *possibility* of this in mind when considering such a problem as the value of breast feeding as compared with bottle feeding. It is true of dynamic psychology in general, but particularly of the psychology of early infancy, that the truth of truths cannot be fully and immediately felt. In other sciences if something is found to be true it can usually be accepted without emotional strain, but in psychology there is always this matter of strain, so that something which is not quite true is more easily accepted than the truth itself.

With this preliminary I would make the bald statement that the relation of the infant to the mother during the breast-feeding orgy is especially intense. Also this relationship is complex, for it has to include the excitement of anticipation, the experience of activity during the feed, as well as the sense of gratification, with rest from instinctual tension resulting from satisfaction. At a later age the sexual group of feelings will rival those that belong to breast feeding of infancy, and the individual will be reminded of the latter when experiencing the former, indeed, the pattern of sexual experience will be found to have derived characteristics and peculiarities from the early infantile instinctual life.

Instinctual moments are not the whole thing, however. There is also the infant's relationship with the mother in the periods in between the orgies of feeding, and excretory experiences which have excitement in them and a climax. There is a tremendous task for the infant in early emotional development, in the bringing together of the two types of relationship to the mother; the one in which instinct is roused, and the other in which the mother is the environment and the provider of the ordinary physical necessities of security, warmth, and freedom from the unpredictable.

Nothing so clearly and satisfactorily establishes the infant's conception of the mother as a whole human being as good experiences during excitement, with gratification and satisfaction. As the infant gradually knows the mother as a whole human being there becomes available a technique for giving her something in return for what she has supplied. The infant thus becomes a total human being too, with a capacity to hold the moment of concern, where something is owed but payment has not yet been made. This is the point of origin of the sense of guilt, and of the infant's capacity to feel sad if the loved mother is away. If a mother succeeds doubly in her relationship to her infant, by establishing satisfactory breast feeding and at the same time by remaining the one person in the infant's life over a period of time until both she and the infant can be felt to be whole human beings, then the emotional development of the infant has gone a long way towards the healthy development which forms the basis eventually for independent existence in a world of human beings. Many mothers feel that they do establish contact with their infants within the first few days, and certainly a baby may be expected after a few weeks to give recognition with a smile. All these things are achievements based on good experiences in maternal care, and in the giving of instinctual gratification; at the beginning these achievements can be lost either by feeding hazards, or difficulties in relation to other instinctual experiences, or else by environmental variability that is beyond the infant's capacity for understanding. The early establishment of the whole human relationships, and the maintenance of these, is of the very greatest value in the development of the child.

It is true, undoubtedly, that a mother who for some reason or other is unable to give breast milk is able to carry through most of this early establishment of a human relationship, giving instinctual gratification at the moments of feeding excitement by the use of a bottle. Nevertheless, by and large, it would appear that mothers who are able to feed by the breast are able to find a much richer experience for themselves in the act of feeding, and this seems to contribute to the early establishment of the relationship as between two human beings. If instinctual gratification were alone the clue then there would be no advantage of breast feeding over bottle feeding. There is, however, the whole attitude of the mother which is of paramount importance.

Further, there is a complication which is of extreme importance in the study of the particular value of breast feeding; *the human infant has ideas.* Every function is elaborated in the psyche, and even at the beginning there is fantasy belonging to the excitement and the experience of feeding. The fantasy, such as it is, is of a ruthless attack on the breast, and eventually on the mother, as the infant becomes able to perceive that it is the mother whose breast is attacked. There is a very strong aggressive element in the primitive love impulse which is the feeding impulse. In terms of the fantasy of a slightly later date the mother is ruthlessly attacked, and although but little aggression may be observable it is not possible to ignore the destructive element in the aim of the infant. Satisfactory feeding finishes off the orgy physically, and also rounds off the fantasy experience; nevertheless there develops a considerable degree of concern on account of the aggressive ideas as soon as the infant begins to put two and two together, and to find that the breast that was attacked and emptied is part of the mother.

The infant who has had a thousand goes at the breast is evidently in a very different condition from the infant who has been fed an equal number of times by the bottle; the survival of the mother is more of a miracle in the first case than in the second. I am not suggesting that there is nothing that the mother who is feeding by bottle can do to meet the situation. Undoubtedly she gets played with by her infant, and she gets the playful bite, and it can be seen that when things are going well the infant almost feels the same as if there is breast feeding. Nevertheless there is a difference. In psycho-analysis, where there is time for a gathering together of all the early roots of the full-blown sexual experience of adults, the analyst gets very good evidence that in a satisfactory breast feed the actual fact of taking from part of the mother's body provides a 'blue-print' for all types of experience in which instinct is involved.

It is a common thing for a baby to be unable to take the breast, not because of any inherent inability, which must be very rare indeed, but because of something which interferes with the mother's capacity to adapt to the baby's needs.[1] Wrong advice to persevere

---

[1] It is interesting in this connection to observe that physiologists now know that milk is not only sucked out of the breast by the infant, but that, in a satisfactory feeding relationship, it is actively secreted from the deeper parts of the mother's breast by physiological processes. The milk in this case actively flows out of the nipple.

However, emotional disturbances in the mother may interfere with these physiological processes, and in this case the infant is only able to obtain milk from the superficial parts of the breast. This active secreting process is known to physiologists as the pumping, expulsion, or ejection reflex. (Editor.)

with breast feeding is notoriously disastrous. A transfer to the bottle produces relief, and it frequently happens that a baby who is in difficulties shows no further difficulty after transfer from the mother's breast to the more impersonal method, that is to say with the bottle intervening. This corresponds to the value that some babies can get from being laid in the cot, because the richness of the experience of actually being held was spoiled by the mother's anxieties, or her depression, which inevitably distort the holding process. From the recognition of the infant's relief at weaning from an anxious or depressed mother it should be possible for the student of the subject to arrive at a theoretical understanding of the great importance that comes from the mother's *positive* ability to fulfil her function in this respect. Success is important to the mother, sometimes more important to her than to the infant, but it is certainly important to the infant also.

It is necessary to add at this point that success in breast feeding does not mean that all problems are thereby smoothed out; success means that a very much more intense and rich experience of relationships is embarked upon, and along with this goes a greater rather than a lesser chance for the infant to produce symptoms which indicate that the really important inherent difficulties that belong to life, and to human relationships, are being met. When bottle feeding has to be substituted there is often an easing in all respects, and, in terms of easy management, a doctor may feel that by easing matters all round he is obviously doing something good. But this is looking at life in terms of ill-health and health. Those who care for infants must be able to think in terms of poverty and richness in the personality, which is quite another thing.

In the case of the breast-fed infant there soon develops a capacity for using certain objects as symbols of the breast, and therefore of the mother. The relationship to the mother (both excited and quiet) is represented in the relationship of the infant to the fist, to a thumb or fingers, or to a bit of cloth, or to a soft toy. There is a very gradual process in the displacement of the aim of the infant's feelings, and an object only comes to stand for the breast when the idea of the breast has been incorporated into the child through actual experiences. It might be thought at first that the bottle could be a breast substitute, but this only makes sense if the bottle is introduced as a plaything at an appropriate time when the infant has had breast experiences. The bottle given instead of the breast, or sub-stituted in the first weeks, has to be a thing on its own account, and to some extent it represents a barrier between the infant and the mother rather than a link. On the whole, bottles are not good breast substitutes.

It is interesting to examine the subject of weaning as it is affected by the alternatives of breast and bottle feeding. Funda-mentally the process of weaning must be the same in the two cases. There arrives a stage in an infant's growth at which there is a play of dropping things, and the mother knows that the infant is reaching a state of development at which weaning can be meaning-ful to him. In this respect there is a readiness for the weaning, no matter whether the breast or the bottle is being used. To some extent, however, no baby is ever ready to be weaned, and this can be said in spite of the fact that in practice a proportion of babies wean themselves. There is always some anger associated with wean-ing, and it is here that the breast and the bottle are so different. In the case of the child who is breast-fed the baby and the mother have to negotiate a period in which there is anger with the breast, and in which there are ideas of an attack not so much motivated by desire as by rage. It is obviously a very much richer experience for the infant and mother to come through this successfully than for them to come through the more mechanical feeding technique, with a bottle as a breast substitute. In the experience of weaning it is an important fact that the mother survives all the feelings belonging to weaning, and she survives partly because the infant protects her, and partly because she can protect herself.

There is a practical problem which assumes great importance in some cases in which a child is to be adopted. Is it better for an infant to have the breast for a little while or not at all? I think the answer to this is not available. In the present state of our knowledge we are not certain whether to advise a mother of an illegitimate baby to feed her baby at the breast or to start off with a bottle, when she knows that an adoption is being arranged. It is held by many that a mother feels very much better about handing over her baby if she has had the chance to give breast feeding, at any rate for a certain length of time; but on the other hand she can be extremely distressed at parting with her infant after such a period. This is a very complex problem, because it may be better for a mother to experience the distress rather than to find afterwards that she was cheated of an experience which she would have welcomed, because it was real. Each case has to be treated on its own merits, with due regard to the feelings of the mother. With regard to the baby, it seems clear that successful breast feeding and weaning provides a good basis for adoption, but it is comparatively rare for a child who is started off so well to be adopted. Much more frequently the beginning of the child's life is *muddled*, so that those who are adopting find themselves with a baby in their care who is already disturbed by having had a complex early history. One thing is certain, that these things do matter very much, and that it is not possible when adopting to ignore the feeding history and the history of general management in the first days and weeks. Processes that are started off easily at those times when all goes well may be very difficult indeed to establish a few weeks or months later when there has been a muddle.

One can say that if a child eventually comes for a long psychotherapy it is better that there shall have been some contact with the breast at the beginning, as this gives a basis of richness of relationships which may possibly be recaptured in the treatment. Nevertheless, most children do not come for psychotherapy, and indeed it is but seldom that prolonged psychotherapy is available; therefore it may be better, when arranging an adoption, to be contented with the poorer start of a reliable bottle-feeding technique, which, by the very fact that it does not so intimately introduce the mother herself, makes it easier for the infant to feel that there is consistent management in spite of the fact that several people are engaged in the feeding process. It seems quite likely that the baby who is bottle fed from the beginning, although poorer for the experience, or perhaps *because* of being poorer for the experience, is able to be fed by a series of minders without too much muddle, simply because at least the bottle and the feed remain constant. Something must be reliable for the infant at the beginning, otherwise there is no hope that he or she may start well on the road to mental health.

A great deal of work needs to be done in this field of enquiry, and it must be acknowledged that the most fruitful source of new understanding is in long-continued psycho-analysis of all types of cases, normal, neurotic, and psychotic, of children of all ages, as well as adults.

In *summary,* it can be said that it is not possible to pass over the matter of a substitute for breast feeding lightly. In some countries and cultures bottle feeding is the rule, and this fact must affect the cultural pattern of the community. Breast feeding provides the richest experience and is the more satisfactory method from the mother's point of view, if it goes well. From the infant's point of view the survival of the mother and her breast after breast feeding is very much more important than the survival of a bottle, and of a mother who gives from a bottle. Difficulties can arise in the mother and the infant as a result of the richness of the experience of breast feeding, but this can hardly be taken as an argument against it, since the aim in infant care is not simply the avoidance of symptoms. The aim of infant care is not limited to the establishment of health, but includes the provision of conditions for the richest possible experience, with long-term results in increased depth and value in the character and personality of the individual.

REFERENCES TO EDITOR'S FOOTNOTE, P. 144

Newton and Newton, *Journal of Paediatrics,* vol. 33, p. 698, 1948.
Cross, *Journal of Endocrinology,* vol. 8a, p. 148, 1952.
Cross, *Journal of Endocrinology,* vol. 9, p. 7, 1953.

4

Why Children Play

[1942]

WHY do children play? Here are some of the reasons, obvious, but perhaps worth reviewing.

Pleasure

Most people would say that children play because they like doing so, and this is undeniable. Children enjoy all physical and emotional play experiences. We can increase the range of both kinds of their experiences by providing materials and ideas, but it seems to be better to provide too little rather than too much of these commodities, since children are able to find objects and invent games very easily, and they enjoy doing so.

To Express Aggression

It is commonly said that children 'work off hate and aggression' in play, as if aggression were some bad substance that could be got rid of. This is partly true, because pent-up resentment and the results of angry experience can feel to a child like bad stuff inside himself. But it is more important to state this same thing by saying that the child values finding that hate or aggressive urges can be expressed in a known environment, without the return of hate and violence from the environment to the child. A good environment, the child would feel, should be able to tolerate aggressive feelings if they are expressed in more or less acceptable form. It must be accepted that aggression is there, in the child's make-up, and the child feels dishonest if what is there is hidden and denied.

Aggression can be pleasurable, but it inevitably carries with it a real or imagined hurting of someone, so that the child cannot avoid having to deal with this complication. To some extent this is dealt with at source, by the child's accepting the discipline or expressing the aggressive feeling in play form and not just when angry. Another way is for aggression to be used in activity that has ultimate constructive aim. But these things are only gradually achieved. It is our part to see that we do not ignore the social contribution the child makes by expressing his aggressive feelings in play instead of at the moment of rage. We may not like being hated or hurt, but we must not ignore what underlies self-discipline in regard to angry impulses.

To Master Anxiety

Whereas it is easy to see that children play for pleasure, it is much more difficult for people to see that children play to master anxiety, or to master ideas and impulses that lead to anxiety if they are not in control.

Anxiety is always a factor in a child's play, and often it is a major factor. Threat of excess of anxiety leads to compulsive play, or to repetitive play, or to an exaggerated seeking for the pleasures that belong to play; and if anxiety is too great, play breaks down into pure exploitation of sensual gratification.

This is not the place to prove the thesis that anxiety underlies children's play. The practical result, however, is important. For in so far as children only play for pleasure they can be asked to give it up, whereas, in so far as play deals with anxiety, we cannot keep children from it without causing distress, actual anxiety, or new defences against anxiety (such as masturbation or day-dreaming).

To Gain Experience

Play is a big part of life for the child. External as well as internal experiences can be rich for the adult, but for the child the riches are to be found chiefly in play and fantasy. Just as the personalities of adults develop through their experience in living, so those of children develop through their own play, and through the play inventions of other children and of adults. By enriching themselves children gradually enlarge their capacity to see the richness of the externally real world. Play is the continuous evidence of creativity, which means aliveness.

Grown-ups contribute here by recognising the big place of play, and by teaching traditional games, yet without cramping or corrupting the children's own inventiveness.

(To-day I would insert here a note on the experience of living in a transitional area of experience, transitional, that is to say, in respect of inner and outer reality. See 'Transitional Objects and Trasitional Phenomena', *Int. J. Psycho-Anal.*, vol. 34, part 2, 1953, and in *The Child and the Family*, p. 31.)

To Make Social Contacts

Children at first play alone, or with mother; other children are not immediately in demand as playmates. It is largely through play, in which the other children are fitted into preconceived roles, that a child begins to allow these others to have independent existence. Just as some adults make friends and enemies easily at work, whereas others may sit in a boarding-house for years and do no more than wonder why no one seems to want them, so do children make friends and enemies during play, while they do not easily make friends apart from play. Play provides an organisation for the initiation of emotional relationships, and so enables social contacts to develop.

Integration of Personality

Play, and the use of the art forms, and religious practice, tend in various but allied ways towards a unification and general integration of the personality. For instance, play can easily be seen to link the individual's relation to inner personal reality with his relation to external or shared reality.

In another way of looking at this highly complex matter, it is in play that the child links ideas with bodily function. It would be profitable, in this connection, to examine masturbation or other sensual exploitation along with the conscious and unconscious fantasy that belongs to it, and to compare this with true playing, in which conscious and unconscious ideas hold sway, and the related bodily activities are either in abeyance or else are harnessed to the play content.

It is when one comes across a case of a child whose compulsive masturbation is *apparently* free of fantasy, or on the other hand a child whose compulsive day-dreaming is *apparently* free from either localised or general bodily excitement, that we recognise most clearly the healthy tendency that there is in play which relates the two aspects of life to each other, bodily functioning and the aliveness of ideas. Play is the alternative to sensuality in the child's effort to keep whole. It is well known that sensuality becomes compulsive, and play becomes impossible, when anxiety is relatively great.

L

Similarly, when one meets with a child in whom the relation to inner reality is unjoined to the relation to external reality; in other words, one whose personality is seriously divided in this respect, we see most clearly how normal playing (like the remembering and telling of dreams) is one of the things that tend towards integration of personality. The child with such serious splitting of the personality cannot play, or cannot play in forms recognisable to others as related to the world.

Communication with People

A child in play may be trying to display at least some of the inside as well as the outside to chosen people in the environment. Play can be 'a being honest about oneself', just as dressing can be for an adult. This can become changed at an early age into its opposite, for play, like speech, can be said to be given us to hide our thoughts, if it is the deeper thoughts that we mean. The repressed unconscious must be kept hidden, but the rest of the unconscious is something that each individual wants to get to know, and play, like dreams, serves the function of self-revelation, and of communication at a deep level.

In psycho-analysis of little children, this desire to communicate through play is used in place of the adult's speaking. The three-year-old child often has a belief in our capacity to understand so great that the psycho-analyst has great difficulty in living up to what the child expects. Great bitterness can follow the child's disillusionment in this respect, and there could be no greater stimulus to the analyst in the search for deeper understanding than the child's distress at our failure to understand what he or she (confidently at first) communicates through play.

Older children are comparatively disillusioned in this respect, and it is no great shock to them to be misunderstood, or even to find that they can deceive, and that education is largely education in deception and compromise. However, all children (even some adults) remain to a lesser or greater degree capable of regaining the belief in being understood, and in their play we can always find the gateway to the unconscious, and to the native honesty which so curiously starts in full bloom in the infant, and then unripens to the bud.

5

The Child and Sex

[1947]

IT is a sign of the times that an article on the child and sex should appear. The need at the present time is for accurate description. As so much is as yet unknown the student is recommended to carry out research in his own way, and if he must read instead of making observations let him read descriptions by many different writers, not looking to one or another as the purveyor of the truth. This article is not the retailing of a set of theories bought wholesale, it is an attempt to put in a few words one person's description of childhood sexuality, based on his training and experience as a paediatrician and psycho-analyst. The subject is vast, and cannot be confined to the limits of an article without suffering distortion.

In considering any aspect of child psychology it is useful to remember that every one has been a child. In each adult observer there is the whole memory of his infancy and childhood, both the fantasy and the reality, in so far as it was appreciated at the time. Much is forgotten but nothing is lost. What better example could direct attention to the vast resources of the unconscious!

In oneself, it is possible to sort out from the vast unconscious the repressed unconscious, and this will include some sexual elements. If special difficulty is found in allowing even for the possibility of childhood sexuality, it is better to turn one's attention to another subject. On the other hand, the observer who is reasonably free to find what is for observation, not having to guard too much (for personal reasons) against finding whatever is to be found, can choose from many different methods for objective study! The most fruitful, and therefore the one necessary for any one who intends to make psychology his life work, is personal analysis, in which (if it is successful) he not only loses the active repressions, but also discovers through memory, and by reliving, the feelings and essential conflicts of his own early life.

THE CONTRIBUTION OF PSYCHO-ANALYSIS

Freud, who was responsible for drawing attention to the importance of childhood sexuality, arrived at his conclusions through the analysis of adults. The analyst has a unique experience every time he conducts a successful analysis, in that he sees unfolding before him the patient's childhood and infancy as it appeared to the patient. He has the repeated experience of getting to see the natural history of a psychological disorder, with all the interweaving of the psychological and the physical, of the personal and the environmental, of the factual and the imagined, of what has been conscious to the patient and what has been under repression.

In analysis of adult men Freud found that the foundations of their sex life and sex difficulties went back to adolescence, and back to childhood, especially to the two- to five-year-old period.

He found that there was a triangular situation which could not be described except by saying that the little boy was in love with his mother, and was in conflict with his father as a sexual rival. The sexual element was proved by the fact that it was not just in fantasy that these things were happening; there were physical accompaniments, erections, excitement phases with climax, murderous impulses, and a specific fear—fear of castration. This central theme was picked out and called the Œdipus complex, and it remains to-day a central fact, infinitely elaborated and modified, but inescapable. Psychology built on a hushing up of this central theme would have been doomed to failure, and therefore one cannot help being grateful to Freud for going ahead and stating what he repeatedly found, bearing the brunt of public reaction.

In using the term Œdipus complex Freud paid tribute to the intuitive understanding of childhood which is independent of psycho-analysis. The Œdipus myth really shows that what Freud wanted to describe has always been known.

A tremendous development of theory has taken place round the nucleus of the Œdipus complex, and much of the criticism of the idea would have been justified if the theory had been put forward as an artist's intuitive understanding of the whole of childhood sexuality or of psychology. But the concept was like a rung in a ladder of scientific procedure. As a concept it had the great merit that it dealt with both the physical and the imaginative. Here was a psychology in which the body and the mind were simply two aspects of one person, essentially related and not to be examined separately without loss of value.

If the central fact of the Œdipus complex is accepted it is immediately possible and desirable to examine the ways in which the concept is inadequate or inaccurate as a clue to child psychology.

The first objection comes from direct observation of little boys. Some boys do express in so many words and quite openly their in-love feeling for their mother and their wish to marry her, and even to give her children, and their consequent hate of father; but many do not express themselves in this way at all, and in fact seem to have more love feeling towards father than towards mother; and in any case brothers and sisters, nurses, and aunts and uncles, easily take the place of the parents. Direct observation does not confirm the degree of importance given to the Œdipus complex by the psycho-analyst. Nevertheless, the psycho-analyst must stick to his guns, because in analysis he regularly finds it, and regularly finds it to be important, and often he finds it severely repressed and only emerging after most careful and prolonged analysis. If, in the observation of children, their games are intimately examined, sexual themes and the Œdipus theme will be regularly found among all the others; but again, the intimate examination of children's games is difficult, and is best done in the course of analysis if it is carried out for research purposes.

The fact seems to be that the full Œdipus situation is but seldom enacted openly in real life. Intimations of it there certainly are, but the tremendously intense feelings associated with periods of instinctual excitement are largely in the child's unconscious or quickly become repressed, being none-the-less real for all that; temper attacks and the common nightmares that occur normally in the three-year-old cannot be understood except in terms of firm attachment to persons, with periodic rising instinctual tension, and acute exacerbation of conflict in the mind arising out of hate and fear clashing with love.

A modification of the original idea (one made by Freud himself) is that the very intense and highly coloured sex situations that an adult in analysis recovers from his own childhood are not necessarily episodes that could have been observed as such by his parents, but nevertheless are true reconstructions based on unconscious feelings and ideas belonging to childhood.

This brings up another point, what about little girls? The first assumption was that they fall in love with their fathers, and hate and fear their mothers. Here again is a truth, and here again the main part is likely to be unconscious, not something that the little girl would admit, except in very special circumstances of trust.

Many girls, however, do not get so far in their emotional development as to become attached to father, and to take the very great risks inherent in being in conflict with mother. Alternatively, an attachment to father is formed, but regression (as it is called) occurs back from a relation to father weakly acquired. The risks inherent in conflict with mother are great indeed, for with the idea of mother (in unconscious fantasy) is associated the idea of loving care, good food, the stability of the earth, and the world in general; and a conflict with mother necessarily involves a feeling of insecurity and dreaming of the ground opening, or worse. The little girl, then, has a special problem, if only because when she comes to love her father her rivalry is with her mother, who is her first love in a more primitive way.

The little girl, like the little boy, has physical sex feelings appropriate to the type of fantasy. It might usefully be said that whereas a boy at the height of his sex wave (at the toddler age and at puberty) is especially afraid of castration, in a girl at a corresponding stage the trouble is a conflict in her relation to the physical world brought about by her rivalry with her mother, who was originally for the child the physical world itself. At the same time the little girl suffers fears in regard to her body, fears of castration like those of a boy, and fears that her body will be attacked by hostile mother figures, in retaliation for her wish to steal her mother's babies, and much else.

BISEXUALITY

This description is obviously defective in respect of bisexuality. At the same time in a child's life that the ordinary heterosexual relationship is vitally important the homosexual relationship always exists, and can be relatively more important than the other. Another way of putting this is to say that a child normally becomes identified with each parent, but at any one moment principally with one parent; and this parent need not be the one of the child's sex. In all cases there is a capacity for identification with the parent of the other sex, so that in the sum total of a child's fantasy life (if search be made) there can be found the whole range of relationships, regardless of the actual sex of the child. It is convenient, naturally, when the main identification is with the parent of the same sex, but in psychiatric examination of a child it would be wrong to jump to a diagnosis of abnormality if the finding is that the child is mainly wanting to be like the parent of the other sex. Such can be the child's natural adaptation to special circumstances. In certain cases cross-identifications can, of course, be a basis for later homosexual tendencies of abnormal quality. In the 'latency' period, between the first sexual period and adolescence, cross-identifications are especially important.

BASIS FOR ADULT MENTAL HEALTH

A principle is being taken for granted in this description which perhaps ought to be deliberately formulated. The basis of sexual health is laid down in childhood, and in the reduplication of early childhood development that takes place at puberty. The corollary is equally true, that sexual aberrations and abnormalities of adult life are laid down in early childhood. Further, the basis of the whole of mental health is laid in early childhood and in infancy—and so is the concern of the paediatrician if he only knew it; but this is an extension of the subject beyond the scope of this article.

SEX IN ORDINARY PLAY

Ordinarily a child's play is greatly enriched by sexual ideas and sexual symbolism, and if there is strong sex-inhibition a play-inhibition follows. There is a possible confusion here arising out of the lack of clear definition of sex play. Sexual excitement is one thing, and the acting out of sex fantasy is another. Sex play with bodily excitement is a special case, and in childhood the outcome is liable to be difficult. The climax or detumescence is often repre-sented more by the aggressive outburst that follows frustration than by a true relief of instinctual tension such as can be obtained by an older person after the onset of puberty. In sleep the dream life rises at times to excited states, and at the climax the body commonly finds some substitute for full sexual orgasm, such as wetting, or waking in nightmare. Sexual orgasm is not likely to be as satisfactory, as such, in the little boy as it can be after puberty, with emission added; perhaps it is more easily got by the little girl who has nothing to add as she matures, except being penetrated. These times of recurring instinctual tension must be expected in childhood, and substitute climaxes have to be provided—notably meals—but also parties, outings, special moments.

Parents know well enough that they often have to step in and induce a climax by a show of strength, even a smack producing tears. Mercifully, children get tired in the end, and go to bed and to sleep. Even so, the delayed climax may disturb the calm of night, as the child wakes in a night-terror, and mother or father is needed immediately if the child is to regain a relation to external reality, and the relief that comes from an appreciation of what is stable in the real world.

All physical excitements have ideational accompaniments, or (the other way round) ideas are themselves the accompaniment of physical experience. Mental pleasure, as well as gratification and relief from tension, comes from the common playing of childhood which is the acting out of fantasy apart from physical excitement. Much of the normal and healthy play of childhood is concerned with sexual ideas and symbolism, and this is not saying that children who are playing are always sexually excited. Children, when playing, may get excited in a general way, and periodically the excitement can become localised and therefore obviously sexual, or urinary, or greedy, or something else based on the capacity of tissues for excitement. Excitement calls for climax. The obvious way out for a child is the game with climax, in which excitement leads to something, 'a chopper to chop off your head', a forfeit, a prize, someone is caught or killed, someone has won, and so on.

Innumerable examples could be given of sex fantasy acted out, but not necessarily accompanied by bodily excitement. It is well known that a big proportion of little girls and some little boys like to play with dolls and to act towards the dolls as mothers do towards babies. They not only do as mother did, thereby complimenting her, but also they do as mother ought to have done, thereby reproaching her. The identification with a mother can be very complete and detailed. As in all these matters, there is a physical side of the experience along with the fantasy that is being acted out, and pains in the belly and sickness can be due to the mother game. Boys as well as girls stick their bellies out for fun, imitating pregnant women, and it is not very uncommon for a child to be brought to the doctor for enlarged belly when the trouble is a secret imitation of a pregnant woman, whose condition is supposed to have been unnoticed. As a matter of fact children are always looking out for swellings, and however successfully sex information is withheld from them they are unlikely to miss spotting a pregnancy. They may, however, keep the information in a compartment of the mind, unassimilated, because of the parents' prudery.

Children the world over have a game called 'Fathers and Mothers', which becomes enriched by an infinite quantity of imaginative material, and the pattern each group of children evolves tells a good deal about the children, and especially about the dominant personality in the group.

Children do often act out the adult type of sexual relationship in relation to each other, but usually this is done secretly and is not therefore recorded by people who are making deliberate observations. Naturally, children easily feel guilty in so playing and also they cannot help being affected by the fact that such play comes under a social ban. It could not be said that these sexual incidents are harmful, but if they are accompanied by a feeling of severe guilt and become repressed, unavailable to the child's consciousness, then harm has been done. This harm can be undone by the recovery of the memory of the incident, and it can sometimes be said that such an incident easily remembered has its value as a stepping-stone in the long and difficult journey from immaturity to maturity.

There are many other sex games which are related less directly to sexual fantasy. No claim is made here that children think only of sex : however, a sex-inhibited child is a poor companion, and is impoverished, like a sex-inhibited adult.

ROOTS OF SEX

The subject of childhood sexuality simply does not allow itself to be confined rigidly to the excitement of sex organs and the fantasy that belongs to such excitement. In studying childhood sexuality it is possible to see the way in which the more specific excitement is built up out of bodily excitements of all types, reaching forward to the more mature feelings and ideas easily recognised as sexual; the more mature develops from the more primitive, the sexual from (for instance) the cannibalistic instinctual urges.

It can be said that a capacity for sexual excitement, in either sex, is present from birth, but the primary capacity of parts of the body for excitement has limited significance until the child's personality has become integrated, and it can be said that it is the child as a whole person who is excited in that specific way. As the infant develops, the sexual type of excitement gradually acquires importance relative to the other types of excitement (urethral, anal, skin, oral), and at the age of 3, 4, or 5 years (as also at puberty) becomes capable, in healthy development, of dominating over other functions in appropriate circumstances.

This is another way of saying that all the innumerable accompaniments of sex in adult behaviour derive from early childhood, and it would be an abnormality and an impoverishment if an adult could not naturally and unselfconsciously employ all manner of infantile or 'pregenital' techniques in sex play. Nevertheless, the compulsion to employ a pregenital *instead of* genital technique in sex experience constitutes perversion, and has its origin in a hold-up of emotional development in early childhood. In analysis of a case of perversion there can always be found both a fear in regard to forward development to mature sex, and a special capacity to get satisfaction in more primitive ways. Sometimes there are actual experiences enticing the child back to infantile types of experience (as when an infant has become excited at introduction of a suppository, or has reacted with excitement to being tightly bound by a nurse, and so on).

The story of the building up of the mature child from the immature infant is long and complex, also it is vitally important for the understanding of the psychology of the adult human being. To develop naturally, the infant and child need an absolutely stable environment.

Roots of female sexuality. The roots of a little girl's sexuality go right down to her early greedy feelings in relation to her mother. There is a gradation from her hungry attack on her mother's body to the mature wish to be like mother. Her love of her father can be as much determined by his being stolen (so to speak) from mother as by his actually being especially loving to her; indeed, when a father is away over the period of a girl's infancy so that she does not really know him, her choice of him as a love object may be entirely due to the fact that he is mother's man. For these reasons there is a close association between stealing and sex desire, and the wish to have a baby.

The consequence of this is that when a woman becomes pregnant and has a baby she has to be able to deal with the feeling, somewhere in her, that the baby was stolen from inside her mother's body. If she cannot feel this, as well as knowing the facts, she loses something of the gratification that pregnancy can bring, and she loses much of the special joy of presenting her own mother with a grandchild. This idea of theft can cause guilt after conception, and can cause miscarriage.

It is especially important to know of this guilt potential in the practical matter of management of the period immediately after child-birth. A mother is at that time very sensitive to the type of woman in charge of her and her baby. She needs help, but because of these ideas derived from early childhood she can only believe in a very friendly or a very hostile mother-figure at that time; and a primipara, even a healthy-minded one, is very liable to feel persecuted by her nurse. The reason for this and other phenomena characteristic of the state of motherhood must be sought in the early roots of the little girl's relation to mother, including her primitive wish to gain womanliness by tearing it from her mother's body.

NATURE OF PSYCHIATRIC ILLNESS

Here is another principle that is worth formulating: in psychiatry every abnormality is a disturbance of emotional development. In treatment, a cure is brought about by enabling the patient's emotional development to go ahead where it was held up. To get to this point where it is held up the patient must always get back to early childhood or infancy, and this fact ought to be of extreme importance to the paediatrician.

Psychosomatic disorders. There is one way in which childhood sexuality is of direct importance to the practising paediatrician; that is, the transformation of sexual excitement into symptoms and physiological changes that resemble the symptoms and changes brought about by physical diseases. These symptoms, which are called psychosomatic, are exceedingly common in all medical practice, and it is from them that the general practitioner weeds out the occasional textbook diseases for the expert attention of the specialist.

These psychsomatic disorders are not seasonal or epidemic; in any one child, however, they show a periodicity, albeit an irregular one. This periodicity is simply an indication of the underlying recurring instinctual tension.

Partly because of internal reasons and partly because of environmental exciting factors, every now and again a child becomes an excitable being. The phrase 'all dressed up and nowhere to go' might have been designed to describe this state. A study of what happens to this excitement is almost a study of childhood, and of the child's problem : how to retain the capacity for eagerness and excitement without experiencing too much painful frustration through lack of satisfactory climax. The main methods by which children cope with this difficulty are :

(a) Loss of capacity for eagerness; but this carries with it a loss of sense of body, and much else that is disadvantageous.

(b) Employment of some sort of reliable climax, either eating or drinking or masturbation, or excited urination or defæcation, or a temper tantrum, or a fight.

(c) The perversion of the body functions in a way that enables a spurious climax to be reached—vomiting and diarrhœa, a bilious attack, exaggeration of a catarrhal infection, complaint of aches and pains that would otherwise be unnoticed.

(d) A general muddle of all these, with a period of unwellness, perhaps with headache and loss of appetite, a period of general irritability, or a tendency of certain tissues to be excitable (for instance, all the phenomena clumped together, in present-day nomenclature, under the word 'allergic').

(e) An organisation of excitement into a chronic 'nerviness' which may remain constant over a long period ('common anxious restlessness', perhaps the most common disorder of child out-patients).

The bodily symptoms and changes related to emotional states and disorders of emotional development form a large and important subject for the attention of the paediatrician.

MASTURBATION

In a description of childhood sexuality, mention must be made of masturbation. Here again is a vast subject for study. Masturbation is either normal or healthy or else it is a symptom of a disorder of emotional development. Compulsive masturbation, just like compulsive thigh-rubbing, nail-biting, rocking, head-banging, head-swaying or rolling, thumb-sucking, and the like, is evidence of anxiety of one kind or another. If severely compulsive it is being employed by the child in his effort to deal with anxiety of more primitive or psychotic type, such as fear of disintegration of personality, or fear of loss of sense of the body, or fear of loss of touch with external reality.

Perhaps the most common disorder of masturbation is its suppression, or its disappearance from a child's repertoire of self-managed defences against intolerable anxiety or sense of deprivation or loss. An infant starts life with the capacity to handle his mouth and to suck his fist, and indeed he needs this ability to comfort himself. He needs his hand to his mouth even if he has what is best for him, a right to his mother's breast when he feels hungry. How much more does he need it when he is regimented. All through infancy he needs whatever satisfaction he can get from his body, from fist-sucking, from passing water, from defæcation, and from holding his penis.

Ordinary masturbation is no more than an employment of natural resources for satisfaction as an insurance against frustration and consequent anger, hate, and fear. Compulsive masturbation simply implies that the underlying anxieties to be dealt with are excessive. Perhaps the infant needs feeding at shorter intervals, or he needs more mothering; or he needs to be able to know that some-one is always near at hand, or his mother is so anxious that she ought to allow him more quiet lying in a pram, and less contact with her. It is logical to try to deal with the underlying anxiety when masturbation is a symptom, but illogical to try to stop the masturbation. It must be recognised, however, that in rare cases compulsive masturbation is continuous and is so exhausting that it has to be stopped by repressive measures, simply in order to give the child some relief from his or her own symptom. When relief is obtained in this way new difficulties must appear in the child's adolescence, but the need for immediate relief can be so great that troubles a few years ahead seem relatively unimportant.

When all goes well, masturbation accompanying sexual ideas

happens without being much noticed, or is only recognised through a child's breathing changes, or because of a sweating head. Trouble follows, however, when there is a combination of compulsion to masturbate with inhibition of sex feeling. In this case the child becomes exhausted by his efforts to produce the satisfaction and climax that he cannot easily attain. To give up involves a loss of sense of reality, or loss of the sense of value. To persist, however, leads eventually to physical debility, and the notorious rings under the eyes which indicate conflict, and which are commonly ascribed wrongly to masturbation itself. Sometimes it is kind to help a child out of this impasse by paternal strictness.

IMPORTANCE OF THE GENITALIA

Psycho-analytic study of children (as of adults) shows that the male genital is valued much more highly in the unconscious than would appear from direct observation, although of course many children do express their interest in the penis openly, if they are allowed. Little boys value their genitalia just as they value their toes and other parts of their bodies, but in so far as they experience sexual excitement they know the penis has special importance. Erection associated with love feelings determines castration fears. The penis excitement of a boy infant has its fantasy parallel, and a great deal depends upon the type of fantasy that goes with the early erections.

The onset of genital excitement is variable. Genital excitement may be almost absent in early infancy or, alternatively, erections may be almost constantly present from birth. Naturally, no good can come from early awakening of penis excitement. It seems likely that the dressings after circumcision frequently stimulate erections and cause an unnecessary association of erection with pain, this being one of several reasons why circumcision should almost never be performed (except on religious grounds). It is convenient when genital excitement is not a marked feature before the other parts of the body have become established as having an importance of their own, and certainly any artificial stimulation of the genitals of infants (either by post-operative procedure or by the desire of uneducated nannies to produce soothing sleep) is a complication; and the process of the child's emotional development is complex enough inherently.

To the little girl the visible and palpable boy's genitalia (scrotum included) are very liable to become an object of envy, but especially in respect of her attachment to her mother developing along iden- tification-with-man lines. However, the matter is not as simple as this, and no doubt a large proportion of little girls are quite con- tented to have their own more hidden but just as important genitalia, and to allow boys their more vulnerable male appendages. In time a girl learns to evaluate the breasts. These become almost as impor- tant to her as the penis is to the boy, and when a girl knows she has the capacity, which a boy has not, to carry and produce as well as to feed babies, she knows she has nothing to envy. Nevertheless, she must envy the boy if she is driven by anxiety back from ordinary heterosexual development to what is called a fixation to her mother, or a mother-figure, with a consequent need to be like a man. Naturally, if a little girl is not allowed or does not allow herself to know she has an exciting and important part of her body in her genitalia, or is not allowed to refer to it, her tendency to penis envy is increased.

Clitoris excitement is closely associated with urinary erotism, which lends itself more to the kind of fantasy that goes with identification with the male. Through clitoris erotism the girl knows what it would feel like to be a boy with penis erotism. Similarly, a boy can experience in the skin of the perineum feelings that correspond to those that belong to the vulva of a girl.

This is quite separate from the anal erotism which is normally a feature in either sex, and provides, along with oral, urethral, muscle, and skin erotism, an early root of sex.

There is no lack of evidence in sociology and folk lore and in the myths and legends of primitive peoples of the paternal or ancestral penis, worshipped in symbolic form and exerting immense influence. In the modern home these things are as important as ever, although they are hidden; but their importance appears when a child's home breaks up, and he suddenly loses the symbols on which he had come to rely, so that he is at sea without a compass, and he is in distress.

CONCLUSION

A child is so much more than sex. In the same way your favourite flower is so much more than water; yet a botanist would fail in his job if in describing a plant he forgot to mention water, of which it is chiefly composed. In psychology there really has been a danger that the sex part of child life might have been left out because of the taboo on childhood sexuality.

The sexual instinct gathers together in childhood, in a highly complex way, out of all its components, and exists as something that enriches and complicates the whole life of the healthy child. Many of the fears of childhood are associated with sexual ideas and excitements, and with the consequent conscious and unconscious mental conflicts. Difficulties of the sexual life of the child account for many psychosomatic disorders, especially those of recurring type.

The basis for adolescent and adult sexuality is laid down in childhood, and also the roots of all sexual perversions and difficulties.

The prevention of adult sexual disorders, as well as of all but the purely hereditary aspects of mental and psychosomatic illness, is in the province of the paediatrician, that is, if the paediatrician can bring himself to study psychology in the way in which he studies physiology and embryology and allied physical sciences.

6

Aggression

[c. 1939]

LOVE and hate form the two chief elements out of which human affairs are built. Both love and hate involve aggression. Aggression, on the other hand, may be a symptom of fear.

It would be a big business to examine all the issues of this preliminary statement, but there are certain relatively simple things to be said about aggression, and these can be brought within the scope of this paper.

I start with an assumption, one which I am aware is not considered by every one to be justified, that whatever good and evil is to be found in the world of human relationships is to be found in the heart of the individual human being. I carry the assumption further, and say that in the infant there is love and hate of full human intensity.

If one thinks in terms of what the infant is organised to withstand, one can easily arrive at the conclusion that love and hate are not experienced more violently by the adult than by the little child.

If all this is accepted, it should follow that we have only to look at the adult human being or at the little child or at the infant, to see the love and hate that are there; but if the problem were as simple as that, there would be no problem. Of all human tendencies aggression, in particular, is hidden, disguised, side-tracked, ascribed to outside agencies, and when it appears it is always a difficult task to trace it to its origins.

Teachers are aware of their pupils' aggressive urges, whether latent or manifest, and every now and again they are forced to deal with aggressive outbreaks or with a child who is aggressive. As I write this I overhear the words, 'She must be suffering from superfluous energy that is not directed into the right channels.' (I write

167

M

this while sitting at ease on a college lawn where teachers are in conference, and some of the teachers' Sunday afternoon conversation drifts my way.)

Here is awareness that instinctual energy that is pent up is a potential danger to the individual and to the community, but when it comes to applying such a truth complications arise which show that there is a lot to be learned about the origins of aggressiveness.

Again the teachers' small talk comes my way, '. . . and do you know what she did last term? She brought me a bunch of violets, so that I was nearly deceived, but I knew she had stolen them from the garden next door! "Render unto Cæsar . . ." I said. Why she steals money and gives sweets to the other children . . .!'

Here, of course, is no simple aggression. The child wants to feel loving, but is hopeless about being able to do so. She just might feel loving for a moment if the teacher or the children could be deceived, but to be worthy of love she must get something from somewhere outside herself.

To understand such a girl's difficulties we have to understand her unconscious fantasies. It is here that we may be sure we can find the aggression that causes her feeling of hopelessness, and therefore that indirectly causes her anti-social attitude. For the aggressive behaviour of children that comes to the attention of a teacher is never a matter solely of emergence of primitive aggressive instincts. No useful theory of childhood aggressiveness can be built on such a false premise.

Before examining fantasy we will search for primary aggression showing in external relationships. How can we get near to this?

We must of course be prepared to find we can never see naked the hate that nevertheless we know exists in the human bosom. Even the little child who wants you to know he likes knocking over bricks only lets you know this because there exists at the moment a general atmosphere of building a tower with the bricks, within which he can be destructive without feeling hopeless.

A rather timid boy of 4 years has attacks of unreasonableness. He shouts at his nurse or mother or father, 'I'll b-burn your h-house d-down! I'll t-tear your insides out! You!'

These attacks are regarded by those who are unfamiliar with them as highly aggressive, and originally they were so. *Magically* they destroy. But in course of time the little boy has come to recognise that the magic fails, and he has transformed the aggressive attacks into orgies in which he enjoys invective with his mouth. His mouth-work over the consonants is terrific. No actual violence is done.

But he does actually wound his parents when he fails to be able to enjoy the presents which they give him. And aggression is effectual when he is taken for a picnic for instance, for owing to his exasperating behaviour every one comes home exhausted. To tire out one's parents is something that the smallest child can do. At first he tires them out without knowing it; then he expects them to like to be tired out by himself; finally he tires them out when he is angry with them.

A little boy of $2\frac{1}{2}$ years is brought to my Clinic because, although he is otherwise a model child, he 'suddenly ups and bites people, even drawing blood'. At times he pulls handfuls of hair out of the heads of those who are caring for him, or he throws crockery on the floor. The spasm over, he is sad about what he has done.

It happens that he only hurts those of whom he is very fond. Chiefly he hurts his mother's mother who is an invalid, and whom he usually cares for just as if he were a grown-up, putting her chair in place, and generally attending to her comfort.

Here is something rather like primary aggression, for the boy is constantly stimulated by both his mother and grandmother, and they feel (quite rightly, to my mind) that he bites 'only when he is excited and simply doesn't know what to do about it'. Just such a glimpse of primary aggression at this age is not very common. The remorse that follows the attacks more usually (by the time a child is this boy's age) takes the form of protecting effectually the people from actual harm. On analysis this boy's attacks would certainly be found to have something more in them than primary aggression.

Encouraged by partial success, let us go to the tiny infant. If an infant should go all out to hurt, not much real harm can be done. Surely the infant can show us naked aggression?

In fact, this is not clearly understood. It is well known that infants do bite their mothers' breasts, even producing blood. They can cause cracked nipples with their gums, and once teeth are present they have the power to do a lot of damage. One mother I know said, 'When the baby was brought to me she went for my breast in a savage way, tore at the nipples with her gums, and in a few moments blood was flowing. I felt torn to pieces and terrified. It took me a long time to recover from the hate roused in me against the little beast, and I think this was a big reason why she never developed real confidence about good food.'

Here is a mother's account of facts revealing her fantasy as well as what may have happened. Whatever this baby really did, it is certain that the majority of infants do not destroy the breasts that are offered them, though we have good evidence that they want to, and even that they believe they do destroy them by feeding from them.

The usual story is that in the course of two or three hundred feeds they bite less than a dozen times. And they bite chiefly when they are excited, and not chiefly when frustrated!

An infant I know, who was born with a lower incisor already cut, and so could have torn the nipple badly, actually suffered partial starvation himself through protecting the breast from damage. Instead of biting the breast the baby chewed on the inside of his lower lip, causing a sore.

It seems that as soon as we admit that the infant can, and has the urge to, hurt, we must admit the existence of an inhibition of aggressive urges making for protection of what is loved and is therefore in danger. Already, soon after birth, infants are unalike in the degree to which they show or hide direct expression of feelings, and it is of some comfort to mothers of angry, screaming babies that the other mother's nice docile infant who sleeps when not fed, and feeds when not asleep, is not necessarily laying down any better foundations for mental health than her own child is doing. It is evidently of value to the developing infant that he has frequently experienced rage at an age when he need not feel remorse. To be angry for the first time at eighteen months must be truly terrifying for the child.

If it is true, then, that the infant has a vast capacity for destruction it is also true that he has a vast capacity for protecting what he loves from his own destructiveness, and the main destruction must always exist in his fantasy. And the important thing to note about this instinctual aggressiveness is that although it soon becomes something that can be mobilised in the service of hate, it is originally a part of appetite, or of some other form of instinctual love. It is something that increases during excitement, and the exercise of it is highly pleasurable.

Perhaps the word *greed* conveys more easily than any other the idea of original fusion of love and aggression, though the love here is confined to mouth-love.

So far I think we have described three things. Firstly there is a theoretical greed or primary appetite-love, which can be cruel, hurting, dangerous, but which is so by chance. The infant's aim is gratification, peace of mind and body. Gratification brings peace, but the infant perceives that to become gratified he endangers what he loves. Normally he compromises, and allows himself enough gratification while not allowing himself to be too dangerous. But to some extent he frustrates himself; so he must hate some part of himself, unless he can find someone outside himself to frustrate him and to bear being hated.

Secondly there comes a separation of what may hurt from what is less likely to hurt. Biting, for instance, can be enjoyed separately from loving people, through the biting of objects that cannot feel. In this way the aggressive elements of appetite can be isolated and saved up for use when the child is angry, and eventually mobilised to combat external reality perceived as bad.

Our search for naked aggression through study of the infant has partially failed, and we must try to profit from our failure. I have already indicated the clue to the reason for our failure, by mentioning the word fantasy.

The truth is that by giving a most minute description of the behaviour of an infant or a child we leave out at least half, for richness of personality is largely a product of the world of inner relationships which the child is all the time building up through taking in and giving out psychically, something which goes on all the while and is parallel to the physical taking in and giving out which is easily witnessed.

The main part of this inner reality, a world felt to be inside the body or within the personality, is unconscious, except in so far as it can be isolated by the individual from the millions of instinctual expressions that have gone to make up its quality.

We see now that here is a field for play of destructive forces which we have not explored, one inside the child's personality, and here indeed we can find (in the course of psycho-analysis, for instance) the good and bad forces at their strongest.

To be able to tolerate all that one may find in one's inner reality is one of the great human difficulties, and an important human aim is to bring into harmonious relationship one's personal inner and outer realities.

Without attempting to go deeply into the origin of the forces that contend for mastery within the personality, I can point out that when the cruel or destructive forces there threaten to dominate over the loving, the individual has to do something to save himself, and one thing he does is to turn himself inside out, to dramatise the inner world outside, to act the destructive role himself and to bring about control by external authority. Control can be established in this way, in the dramatised fantasy, without serious damping down of instincts, whereas the alternative, control within, would need to be generally applied, and would result in a state of affairs known clinically as depression.

When there is hope in regard to the inside things, instinctual life is active, and the individual can enjoy using instinctual urges, including aggressive ones, in making good in real life what has been hurt in fantasy. This forms the basis for both play and work. It can be seen that in applying the theory one is limited in the amount one can help a child on the road to sublimation by the state of the child's inner world. If destruction there is excessive and unmanageable, very little reparation is possible and we can do nothing to help. All that the child can do is either to deny ownership of bad fantasies or to dramatise them.

Aggressiveness, which presents a serious problem of management to the teacher, is nearly always this dramatisation of inner reality which is too bad to be tolerated as such. Often it implies a breakdown of masturbation or of sensuous exploitation which, when successful, provides a link between outer and inner reality, between bodily senses and fantasy (though the fantasy is mainly unconscious fantasy). It has been pointed out that there is a relation between the giving up of masturbation and onset of anti-social behaviour (recently mentioned by Anna Freud in an unpublished lecture) and the cause of this relationship is to be found in the attempt of the child to bring an inner reality that is too terrible to be acknowledged into relation with external reality. Masturbation and dramatisation provide alternative methods, but each must fail in its object, because the only true link is the relation of inner reality to the original instinctual experiences that built it up. This relationship can only be traced by psycho-analytic treatment, and as the fantasy is too terrible to be accepted and tolerated it cannot be used in sublimation.

Normal individuals are always doing what abnormal ones can only do by analytic treatment, that is, altering their inner selves by new experiences of intake and output. It is a constant problem of children and adults to find safe ways of disposing of badness. Much is dramatised and dealt with (falsely) through care over disposal of physical elements that come from the body. Another method is by means of games or work which involve distinctive action which can be enjoyed, with consequent lifting of the sense of frustration and grievance : a boy boxing or kicking a football feels better for what he is doing, partly because he has enjoyed hitting and kicking, and partly because he unconsciously feels (falsely) that he has driven badness out of his fists and feet.

A girl who longs for a baby to some extent longs for the reassurance that she has taken in something good, has retained it, and has something good developing inside her. This is a reassurance she needs (though it is a false one) because of her unconscious feeling that she may be empty, or full of bad things. It is her aggression that gives her these ideas. She also, of course, seeks the peace she feels she may get if instinctually gratified, which means she fears the aggressive elements of her appetite which threaten to dominate her if she is frustrated during excitement. Masturbation can help in the latter need, but not in the former.

Following this, it can be seen that environmental hate or frustration arouses manageable or unmanageable reactions in the individual according to the amount of tension that already exists in the individual's personal unconscious fantasy.

Another important method for dealing with aggression in the inner reality is the masochistic one by which the individual finds suffering, and by one stroke expresses aggression, gets punished and so relieved of guilt feelings, and enjoys sexual excitement and gratification. This is outside the present subject.

Secondly there is the management of fear-driven aggression, the dramatised version of a too-awful inner world. The object of this aggression is to seek out control, and to compel it to function. It is the adult's job to prevent this aggression from becoming out of hand by provision of confident authority, within the bounds of which some degree of badness can be dramatised and enjoyed without danger. The gradual withdrawal of this authority is an important part of the management of adolescents, and adolescent boys and girls can be grouped according to their capacity to stand withdrawal of imposed authority.

It is the task of parents and teachers to see that children never meet so weak an authority that they run amok, or that they must, from fear, take over the authority themselves. Anxiety-driven assumption of authority is dictatorship, and those who have made the experiment of letting children control their own destinies know that the calm adult is less cruel as a manager than a child quickly becomes when he is responsible for too much.

Thirdly (and here sex makes a difference), there is the management of mature aggressiveness, that which is clearly seen in adolescent boys and which to a large extent motivates adolescent competition in games and work. Potency involves toleration of the idea of killing a rival (which leads to the problem of the value of the idea of war, an unpopular subject).

Mature aggressiveness is not something to be cured; it is something to be noted and allowed for. If it is unmanageable, we jump aside, and the law takes over. The law is learning to respect adolescent aggression, and the country counts on it in wartime.

Finally, all aggression that is not denied, and for which personal responsibility can be accepted, is available to give strength to the work of reparation and restitution. At the back of all play, work, and art, is unconscious remorse about harm done in unconscious fantasy, and an unconscious desire to start putting things right.

Sentimentality contains an unconscious denial of the destructiveness underlying construction. It is withering to the developing child, and eventually it can make him need to show in direct form destructiveness which, in a less sentimental milieu, he could have conveyed indirectly by showing a desire to construct.

It is partly false to state that we 'should provide opportunity for creative expression if we are to counter children's destructive urges'. What is needed is an unsentimental attitude towards *all* productions, which means the appreciation not so much of talent as of the struggle behind all achievement, however small. For, apart from sensual love, no human manifestation of love is felt to be valuable that does not imply aggression acknowledged and harnessed.

An aim in personality-building is to become able to tap more and more of the instinctual. This involves becoming more and more able to acknowledge one's own cruelty and greed, which can then, and only then, be harnessed to sublimated activity.

Only if we know the child wants to knock the tower of bricks down is it a valuable thing for him if we see that he can build it up.

The Impulse to Steal

[1949]

I T seems to me that there is something that the ordinary parent
wants to know about thieving. A statement is needed which
joins up the ordinary primitive love impulses of the little child
with the compulsive acts of the older child, and of the adult. Of
course, any explanation that can be made in a few words must
be too simple. For instance, when an older child has a compulsion
to steal there may very likely be a hallucinated dominant person,
or voice, that directs him, and this sort of complexity has to be left
out, if a general statement is to be formulated. On the understanding that a great deal is being left out, I find it useful to put the
psychology of stealing in the following way.

Simplified Statement of the Impulse to Steal

There are degrees of stealing.

When a child takes something and enjoys it we do not find ourselves wanting to use the word thief. If a child goes over the wall
and takes a ripe apple and eats it and enjoys it, we feel that he
is very much like any other boy, and also that he is like the small
child who reaches for something on the table which has an exciting
colour or shape, regardless of whether it has been offered to him
or not. The older child who gets over into the orchard and
takes green apples, eats them rather quickly, and then gets stomach
ache, is obviously acting a little under the stress of anxiety. This is
the very slightest degree of thieving. If he is sick afterwards, this
may be due to the sourness of the apples, or to guilt, or maybe to
both these things. This is a little nearer to thieving.

A child who, time after time, goes and steals apples, and quickly
gives them away without himself enjoying them, is acting under a

compulsion, and is ill. He can be called a thief. He will not know why he has done what he has done, and if pressed for a reason he will become a liar. The thing is, what is this boy doing? (Certainly the thief may be a girl, but it is clumsy to use both pronouns each time.) *The thief is not looking for the object that he takes. He is looking for a person. He is looking for his own mother, only he does not know this.* To the thief it is not the fountain pen from Woolworths, or the bicycle from the neighbour's railings, or the apple from the orchard, that can give satisfaction. A child who is ill in this way is incapable of enjoying the possession of things stolen. He is only acting out a fantasy which belongs to his primitive love impulses, and the best he can do is to enjoy the acting out, and the skill exercised. The fact is that he has lost touch with his mother in some sense or other. The mother may or may not still be there. She may even be there, and a perfectly good mother, and able to give him any amount of love. From the child's point of view, however, there is something missing. He may be fond of his mother and even in love with her, but, in a more primitive sense, for some reason or other she is lost to him. The child who is thieving is an infant looking for the mother, or for the person *from whom he has a right to steal;* in fact, he seeks the person from whom he can take things, just as, as an infant and a little child of 1 or 2 years old, he took things from his mother simply because she *was* his mother, and because he had rights over her.

There is one further point; *his own mother is really his, because he invented her.* The idea of her arose gradually out of his own capacity to love. We may know that Mrs. So-and-so, who has had six children, at a certain time gave birth to this baby Johnny, and that she fed him and looked after him, and then eventually had another child. From Johnny's point of view, however, when he was born this woman was something he created; by actively adapting herself to his needs, she showed him what it would be sensible to create, as it was actually there. What his mother gave to him of herself had to be conceived of, had to be *subjective* for him before *objectivity* began to mean anything. Ultimately, in the tracing down of thieving to its roots, it can always be found that the thief has a need to re-establish his relation to the world on the basis of a refind-ing of the person who, because she is devoted to him, understands him and is willing to make an active adaptation to his needs; in fact to give him the illusion that the world contains what he can conceive of, and to enable him to place this that he conjures up just where there actually is a devoted person in external 'shared' reality.

What is the practical application of this? The point is that the healthy infant in each one of us only gradually becomes able to perceive objectively the mother whom at first he created. This painful process is what is called disillusionment, and there is no need actively to disillusion a small child; rather can it be said that the ordinary good mother holds back disillusionment, and allows it only in so far as she feels the infant can take it, and welcome it.

A two-year-old child who is stealing pennies from mother's handbag is playing at being a hungry infant who thought he created his mother, and who assumed that he had rights over her and her contents. Disillusionment can come only too quickly. The birth of a new baby, for instance, can be a terrible shock just in this particular way even when the child is prepared for his or her advent and even when there is good feeling towards the new baby. The sudden access of disillusionment in respect of a little child's feeling that he created his own mother which the advent of the new baby can cause, easily starts a phase of compulsive stealing. Instead of playing at having full rights over his mother, the child may be found to be compulsively taking things, especially sweet things, and hiding them, but without really getting satisfaction from having them. If parents understand what this phase of a more compulsive type of stealing means they will act sensibly. They will tolerate it, for one thing, and they will try to see that the child whose nose has been put out of joint can at least rely on a certain quantity of special personal attention, at a certain time each day; and the time for starting the weekly penny may have arrived. Above all, parents who understand this situation will not come down like a ton of bricks on the child and demand confession. They will know that if they do so the child will certainly start lying as well as thieving, and it will be absolutely their fault.

These are common matters in ordinary healthy households, and in the vast majority of cases the whole thing is got through sensibly, and the child who is temporarily under compulsion to steal things recovers.

There is a vast difference, however, according to whether parents understand enough about what is happening to avoid unwise action, or whether they feel they must 'cure' the thieving in its early stages, in order to prevent the child from becoming a confirmed thief at a later date. Even when things eventually go well the amount of unnecessary suffering which children undergo through mismanagement of this sort of detail is tremendous. The essential suffering is sufficient indeed. It is not only in respect of thieving. In all sorts of ways children who have suffered some too great or sudden access of disillusionment find themselves under a compulsion to do things without knowing why, to make messes, to refuse to defæcate at the correct moment, to cut the heads off the plants in the garden, etc.

Parents who feel they must get to the bottom of these acts, and who ask children to explain why they have done what they have done, are vastly increasing the children's difficulties, which are already intense enough just then. A child cannot give the real reason, not knowing it, and the result may be that, instead of feeling almost unbearable guilt as a result of being misunderstood and blamed, he will become split in his person; split into two parts, one terribly strict, and the other possessed by evil impulses. The child then no longer feels guilty, but is instead being transformed into what people will call a liar.

The shock of having one's bicycle stolen is not, however, mitigated by the knowledge that the thief was unconsciously looking for his mother. This is altogether another kettle of fish. Revenge feelings in the victim can certainly not be ignored, and any attempt to be sentimental about delinquent children defeats its own aim by raising the tension of general antagonism towards criminals. Magistrates in a juvenile court cannot only think of the thief as ill, and cannot ignore the anti-social nature of the delinquent act, and the irritation which this must engender in the localised bit of society which is affected. Indeed we are putting a tremendous strain on society when we ask the courts to recognise the fact that a thief is ill, so that treatment rather than punishment may be prescribed.[1]

There is of course much stealing which never comes into the courts, because it is dealt with satisfactorily in the home of the child by ordinary good parents. One can say that a mother feels no strain when her small child is stealing from her, as she would never dream of calling this stealing, and she easily recognises that what the child

[1] See 'Some Psychological Aspects of Juvenile Delinquency' p. 181.

is doing is an expression of love. In the management of the four- and five-year-old child, or the child who is passing through a phase in which there is a certain amount of compulsive stealing, there is certainly some strain on the parents' tolerance. We should give these parents anything that we can give in the way of understanding of the processes involved, in order to help them to carry their own children through to social adjustment. It is for this reason that I have tried to put down one person's point of view, deliberately simplifying the problem in order to present it in a form that can be understood by the good parent or teacher.

Summary of Views Expressed

The infant who quite ordinarily and healthily claims possession of his mother, and who purloins whatever attracts him, is basking in the *illusion* that he created whatever interests him in the world's shop window. The young child who quite commonly does a bit of compulsive stealing from mother's handbag, and from the food cupboard, is reacting to a jerk forward in the painful process of *disillusionment*.

The thief, an ill person, is most of the time hopeless about the world and its relation to himself. Periodically, however, he gets a wave of hope, and this takes the form of an attempt to *get behind the disillusionment process;* the infant self, with memories of basking in illusion and in subjectivity unchallenged, comes to life, and for a brief spell inhabits the child's person. The result from our point of view is that this person, child, adolescent or adult, acts as one possessed, possessed by one aspect of his infant self, compelled to steal to make contact with society.

8

Some Psychological Aspects of Juvenile Delinquency [1]

[1946]

I FIND I want to give a simple and yet not untrue description of one aspect of delinquency, a description that links delinquency with deprivation of home life. This could prove helpful to those who wish to understand the roots of the delinquent's problem.

First I invite consideration of the word unconscious. This talk is addressed to magistrates, who are, by training, accustomed to weighing up evidence, to thinking things out as well as feeling things. Now Freud contributed something really useful here. He showed that if we substitute thinking-out for feeling we cannot leave out the unconscious without making gross errors; in fact not without making fools of ourselves. The unconscious may be a nuisance for those who like everything tidy and simple, but it definitely cannot be left out of account by planners and thinkers.

Man the feeler, man the intuitive, far from leaving the unconscious out of account, has always been swayed by his unconscious. But man the thinker has not yet realised that he can both think and also at the same time include the unconscious in his thinking. Thinking people, having tried logic and having found it shallow, have started on a reaction towards unreason, which is a dangerous tendency indeed. The strange thing is to what a degree front-rank thinkers, even scientists, have failed to make use of this particular scientific advance. Do we not see economists leaving out of account unconscious greed, politicians ignoring repressed hate, doctors unable to recognise the depression and hypochondria that underlie such illnesses as rheumatism and that impair the industrial machine? We

[1] An address given by invitation to magistrates.

even have magistrates who fail to see that thieves are unconsciously looking for something more important than bicycles and fountain pens.

Every magistrate is fully aware of the fact that thieves have unconscious motives. First, however, I want to state and emphasise quite a different application of the same principle. I want to ask for consideration of the unconscious in its relation to the job of being a magistrate, this job being the implementing of the law.

It is because I am so anxious to see psychological methods used in the investigation of court cases, and in the management of anti-social children, that I want to make an attack on one of the biggest threats to an advance in that direction; this threat comes from the adoption of a sentimental attitude towards crime. If advances seem to come but are based on sentimentality, they are valueless; reaction must surely set in, and the advances had better never have been made. In sentimentality there is repressed or unconscious hate, and this repression is unhealthy. Sooner or later the hate turns up.

Crime produces public revenge feelings. Public revenge would add up to a dangerous thing were it not for the law and those who implement it. First and foremost in court work, the magistrate gives expression to public revenge feelings, and only by so doing can the foundation be laid for a humane treatment of the offender.

I find that there can be very strong resentment over this idea. Many people, if asked, may claim that they do not want to punish criminals, that they would rather see them treated. But my suggestion, one based on very definite premises, is that no offence can be committed without an addition being made to the general pool of unconscious public revenge feelings. It is one function of the law to protect the criminal against this same unconscious, and therefore blind, revenge. Society feels frustrated, but it allows the offender to be dealt with in the courts, after the passage of time and the cooling of passion; some satisfaction follows when justice is done. There is a real danger lest those who want to see offenders treated as ill people (as they are indeed) will be thwarted just as they are seeming to succeed, through not taking into account the unconscious revenge potential. There would be danger in the adoption of a purely therapeutic aim on the magisterial bench.

This having been said, I can go on to what interests me so very much more, the understanding of crime as a psychological illness.

t is a huge and complex subject, but I will try to say something imple about anti-social children, and the relation of delinquency o deprivation of home life.

You know that in investigation of the several pupils in an pproved school diagnosis may range from normal (or healthy) to chizophrenic. However, something binds together all delinquents. What is it?

In an ordinary family, a man and woman, husband and wife, ake joint responsibility for their children. Babies are born, mother supported by father) brings each child along, studying the per- onality of each, coping with each one's personal problem as it ffects society in its smallest unit, the family and the home.

What is the normal child like? Does he just eat and grow and mile sweetly? No, that is not what he is like. A normal child, if he has confidence in father and mother, pulls out all the stops. In the course of time he tries out his power to disrupt, to destroy, to frighten, to wear down, to waste, to wangle, and to appropriate. Everything that takes people to the courts (or to the asylums, for that matter) has its normal equivalent in infancy and early childhood, in the relation of the child to his own home. If the home can stand up to all the child can do to disrupt it, he settles down to play; but business first, the tests must be made, and especially so if there is some doubt as to the stability of the parental set-up and the home (by which I mean so much more than house). At first the child needs to be conscious of a framework if he is to feel free, and if he is to be able to play, to draw his own pictures, to be an irresponsible child.

Why should this be? The fact is that the early stages of emotional development are full of potential conflict and disruption. The rela- tion to external reality is not yet firmly rooted; the personality is not yet well integrated; primitive love has a destructive aim, and the small child has not yet learned to tolerate and cope with instincts. He can come to manage these things, and more, if his surroundings are stable and personal. At the start he absolutely needs to live in a circle of love and strength (with consequent tolerance) if he is not to be too fearful of his own thoughts and of his imaginings to make progress in his emotional development.

Now what happens if the home fails a child before he has got the idea of a framework as part of his own nature? The popular

N

idea is that, finding himself 'free' he proceeds to enjoy himself. This is far from the truth. Finding the framework of his life broken he no longer feels free. He becomes anxious, and if he has hope he proceeds to look for a framework elsewhere than at home. The child whose home fails to give a feeling of security looks outside his home for the four walls; he still has hope, and he looks to grandparents, uncles and aunts, friends of the family, school. He seeks an external stability without which he may go mad. Provided at the proper time, this stability might have grown into the child like the bones in his body, so that gradually in the course of the first months and years of his life he would have passed on to independence from dependence and a need to be managed. Often a child gets from relations and school what he missed in his own actual home.

The anti-social child is merely looking a little farther afield, looking to society instead of to his own family or school to provide the stability he needs if he is to pass through the early and quite essential stages of his emotional growth.

I put it this way. When a child steals sugar he is looking for the good mother, his own, from whom he has a right to take what sweetness is there. In fact this sweetness is his, for he invented her and her sweetness out of his own capacity to love, out of his own primary creativity, whatever that is. He is also looking for his father, one might say, who will protect mother from his attacks on her, attacks made in the exercise of primitive love. When a child steals outside his own home he is still looking for his mother, but he is seeking with more sense of frustration, and increasingly needing to find at the same time the paternal authority that can and will put a limit to the actual effect of his impulsive behaviour, and to the acting out of the ideas that come to him when he is in a state of excitement. In full-blown delinquency it is difficult for us as observers, because what meets us is the child's acute need for the strict father, who will protect mother when she is found. The strict father that the child evokes may also be loving, but he must first be strict and strong. Only when the strict and strong father figure is in evidence can the child regain his primitive love impulses, his sense of guilt, and his wish to mend. Unless he gets into trouble, the delinquent can only become progressively more and more inhibited in love, and consequently more and more depressed and depersonalised, and eventually unable to feel the reality of things at all, except the reality of violence.

Delinquency indicates that some hope remains. You will see that it is not *necessarily* an illness of the child when he behaves anti-socially, and anti-social behaviour is at times no more than an S.O.S. for control by strong, loving, confident people. Most delinquents are to some extent ill, however, and the word illness becomes appropriate through the fact that in many cases the sense of security did not come into the child's life early enough to be incorporated into his beliefs. While under strong management, an anti-social child may seem to be all right; but give him freedom and he soon feels the threat of madness. So he offends against society (without knowing what he is doing) in order to re-establish control from outside.

The normal child, helped in the initial stages by his own home, grows a capacity to control himself. He develops what is sometimes called an 'internal environment', with a tendency to find good surroundings. The anti-social, ill child, not having had the chance to grow a good 'internal environment', absolutely needs control from without if he is to be happy at all, and if he is to be able to play or work. In between these two extremes of normal and anti-social ill children are children who can still achieve a belief in stability if a continuous experience of control by loving persons can be given them over a period of years. A child of 6 or 7 stands a much better chance of getting help in this way than one of 10 or 11.

In the war many of us had experience of just this belated provision of a stable environment for children deprived of home life, in the hostels for evacuated children, especially for those who were difficult to billet. These have been under the Ministry of Health. In the war years, children with anti-social tendencies were treated as ill. I am glad to say these hostels are not all closing down now, and they have been transferred to the care of the Ministry of Education. These hostels do prophylactic work for the Home Office. They can treat delinquency *as an illness* the more easily because most of the children have not yet come before the Juvenile Courts. Here, surely, is the place for the treatment of delinquency as an illness of the individual, and here, surely, is the place for research, and opportunity to gain experience. We all know the fine work done in some approved schools, but the fact that most of the children in them have been convicted in a court makes for difficulty.

In these hostels, sometimes called boarding-homes for maladjusted children, there is an opportunity for those who see anti-social behaviour as the S.O.S. of an ill child to play their part, and so to learn. Each hostel or group of hostels under the Ministry of Health in wartime had a committee of management, and in the group with which I was connected the lay committee really interested itself in, and took responsibility for, the details of the hostel work. Surely many magistrates could be elected to such committees, and so get into close contact with the actual management of children who have not yet come before the Juvenile Courts. It is not enough to visit approved schools or hostels, or to hear people talking. The only interesting way is to take some responsibility, even if indirectly, by intelligently supporting those who manage boys and girls who tend towards anti-social behaviour.

In such hostels for the so-called maladjusted one is free to work with a therapeutic aim, and this makes a lot of difference. Failures will eventually come to the courts, but successes become citizens.

Of course, the work done in these small and properly staffed hostels is done by the wardens. These wardens have to start as the right kind, but they need education and opportunities for discussing their work as they go along, and also they need someone in between them and that impersonal thing called a ministry. In the scheme I knew, this was the job of the psychiatric social worker and the psychiatrist. These in turn needed a committee which could grow with the scheme, and profit from experience. It is on this sort of committee that a magistrate could profitably serve.

Now to return to the theme of children deprived of home life. Apart from being neglected (in which case they reach the Juvenile Courts as delinquents) they can be dealt with in two ways. They can be given personal psychotherapy, or they can be provided with a strong stable environment with personal care and love, and gradually increasing doses of freedom. As a matter of fact, without this latter the former (personal psychotherapy) is not likely to succeed. And with the provision of a suitable home-substitute, psychotherapy may become unnecessary, which is fortunate because it is practically never available. It will be years before properly-trained psycho-analysts are available even in moderate numbers for giving the personal treatments that are so urgently needed in many cases.

Personal psychotherapy is directed towards enabling the child to complete his or her emotional development. This means many things, including establishing a good capacity for feeling the reality of real things, both external and internal, and establishing the integration of the individual personality. Full emotional development means this and more. After these primitive things, there follow the first feelings of concern and guilt, and the early impulses to make reparation. And in the family itself there are the first triangular situations, and all the complex interpersonal relationships that belong to life at home.

Further, if this all goes well, and if the child becomes able to manage himself and his relationship to grown-ups and to other children, he still has to begin dealing with complications, such as a mother who is depressed, a father with maniacal episodes, a brother with a cruel streak, a sister with fits. The more we think of these things the more we understand why infants and little children absolutely need the background of their own family, and if possible a stability of physical surroundings as well; and from such considerations we see that children deprived of home life must either be provided with something personal and stable when they are yet young enough to make use of it to some extent, or else they must force us later to provide stability in the shape of an approved school, or, in the last resort, four walls in the shape of a prison cell.

INDEX

Acting out, 158–9
Adaptation, to child's needs, 7, 136
Adoption, 45ff., 52ff.
  and breast feeding, 146–7
Aggression, 17, 69, 102, 144, 167ff.
  play and, 149–50
  primary, 168–9
Anger,
  and weaning, 146
  in infancy, 170
Anti-social behaviour, 117
Anxiety, 132
  masturbation and, 163
  play and, 150
Authoritarianism, 70–1
Authority, withdrawal of, 174

Baby, physical care of, 138
Bathing baby, 135
Bed-wetting, 100
Behaviour, changes in, 22
Biology, 40, 43
Bisexuality, 156–7
Biting, 171
Blood relationship, value of, 11
Bottle feeding, 140, 143, 145ff.
Bowlby, Dr John, 10
Breast,
  girl's attitude to, 165
  symbols of, 145
Breast feeding, 141ff.

Castration fear, 156, 164
Circumcision, 164
Classification of children, 31–4,
  108–9
Climaxes, substitute, 158
Clitoris excitement, 164
Conscience, 132
Corporal punishment, 106 and n.

Darwin, 129
Delinquency, 100ff.
  and deprivation, 183ff.
  prevention of, 120–1
  psychology of, 181ff.

Dependence, of infant on mother,
  7
Depression, 172
Destructiveness, see Aggression
Diagnosis, 29, 72
  in education, 30ff., 35
'Difficult' children, 98ff.
Disillusionment, 140, 178, 180
Dramatisation, 172–4
Dreams, 4, 130

Education, war news and, 73–4
Environment, internal, 185
Evacuation, 75ff., 83ff., 98ff.,
  117ff.
  reasons for, 76
  return from, 88ff.
Excitement, childhood, 162
Excretion, as relationship, 139
Experience, play and, 150

Family pattern, changing, 7, 8ff.
Fantasy,
  infantile, 144
  sex, in children, 158–9
  unconscious, 74
Father,
  role at nursery school age, 15
  strict, 184
'Fathers and mothers', game, 6, 159
Fearfulness, 38
Feeding,
  and human relationships, 25
  at nursery school, 19
  successful, 139
  see also Breast feeding; Bottle
    feeding
Feelings,
  expression of child's, 16
  infant's, 141
  loss of, 86
  primitive, 128
Foster homes, 10, 12, 79
  see also Adoption; Evacuation
Freedom, child's view of, 70

Freud, Anna, 172
Freud, Sigmund, 129, 130, 131, 154, 181
Friends, 109
Frustrations, teacher's, 27–8

Games, sexual themes in, 155–9
Gangs, 109
Genitalia, 164–5
Girls, sexuality in little, 156
Gratification, 171
Greed, 171
Grief, 36
Growth, conditions for, 3ff.
Guilt feelings, 17, 42, 143
    and pregnancy, 161

Hate,
    and play, 149
    in four-year-old, 4, 5
Head-banging, 47–50
Health, promotion of, 9
Help, for parents, 8
History-taking, 35–6, 39, 108
Home,
    and four-year-old, 4
    child's relation to, 94–7
    relation to school, 31–3
Home experiences, primary, 102
Homosexuality, 156–7
Hostels, 32, 101ff., 117ff., 185–6
    placing in, 120
    staff of, 111–12, 118–19
Human nature, study of, 125ff.
Hypnotism, 131

Id, 132
Ideas, in infant, 144
Identification, 3–4
    cross-, 157
    with parents, 157
Illegitimate children, 42
Incontinence, 17, 27, 100
Individualists, parents as, 8
Influence, 25ff.
Insanity, 104

Instinct, 4
    in nursery-school-age child, 16
Integration of child, 18, 151
Intelligence Tests, 30
Interference, protection from, 13
Intuition, and science, 127
Isaacs, Susan, 12

Jealousy, 79
Job, parenthood as a, 8–9
Judgment, parents', 10

Latency period, 70, 157
Leaderless groups, 99n.
Logic, 132
Love, child's need of, 7
Love and hate, in children, 16, 17, 102, 167ff.
Lying, 177, 178

McMillan, Margaret, 12
Management, teachers and, 32
Masochism, 173
Masturbation, 41, 151, 162–4, 172, 173
Maturity,
    and health, 134
    of under-fives, 5
Milk, secretion of, 144
Mother,
    and physical care of child, 7
    deprived, 75ff.
    how needed, 138
Mother fixation, 165
'Mothering', 137

Needs, emotional, of children, 31
Nightmares, 155
Nurseries, day, 11–13
Nursery Schools, 12, 14ff.

Œdipus complex, 154–5
Orgasm, 158

Pædiatrics, 9–10

INDEX

Parents,
  and four-year-olds, 4
  identification with, 157
Penis, importance in childhood, 164–5
Perception, 17
Persecution, 37–8
Person, baby as, 135ff.
Perversion, sexual, 160
Picking up baby, 135, 136
Play, 6, 21, 22
  reasons for, 149ff.
  sex in, 157–8
Pregnancy,
  and guilt feelings, 161
  children and, 159
  in girls, 42
P.S.W., 104, 106, 107
Psycho-analysis, 125ff., 147
  and childhood sexuality, 154ff.
Psychology, meaning of, 125
Psychoses, 133
Psychosomatic illness, 161–2
Psychotherapy, and hostels, 119, 186–7
Puberty, 71

Reality,
  internal and external, 152, 172
  introduction to, 139
Regression, 156
Relationship(s),
  mother's, to baby, 137
  play and, 151
  teacher-pupil, 27, 85
  triangular, 5–6, 16
  two-person, 6
Reparation, 17, 174
  excretion and, 139
Repression, 130–1
Residential management, 98ff.
Restlessness, 162
Revenge feelings, 182

School(s),
  child's relation to, 31–2
  private and State, 33

Science, 127
Security, 114
Self, and external world, 5, 21
Sensuality, and play, 151
Sentimentality, 174, 182
Separation, from mother, 10
Sex,
  and infantile instinctual life, 142
  and play, 157–8
  children and, 40ff., 153ff.
  pregenital technique in, 160
Sex talks, 40–1
Sexuality,
  childhood, 153ff.
  female, origins, 160–1
Shakespeare, 126
Shyness, 37, 38
Siblings, lack of, 11–12
Social sense, in children, 42
Society, and responsibility for children, 9–10
Stability, 110–11, 183–5
Stealing, impulse to, 176ff.
Strain, in psychology, 142
Super-ego, 132–3

Teach, drive to, 26
Teachers, nursery school, 15, 19ff.
  relationship with mother, 19
Teaching, and diagnosis, 30ff.
Temper tantrums, 155
Thieving, 176ff.

Unconscious, 24ff., 130–1, 132, 152, 153, 181

Vaccination, 138

War,
  and character types, 72–3
  children and, 69ff.
Wardens, 105–6, 186
  qualifications of, 112–13
  see also Hostels
Weaning, 18, 140, 145, 146–7

THE END